Joseph Solomon Moore

The Champion Tariff Swindle of the World

Joseph Solomon Moore

The Champion Tariff Swindle of the World

ISBN/EAN: 9783744723954

Printed in Europe, USA, Canada, Australia, Japan

Cover: Foto ©ninafisch / pixelio.de

More available books at **www.hansebooks.com**

QUESTIONS OF THE DAY. NO. L.

The Champion Tariff Swindle of the World

FRIENDLY LETTERS

TO

AMERICAN FARMERS

AND OTHERS

By J. S. MOORE

NEW YORK AND LONDON
G. P. PUTNAM'S SONS
1888

CONTENTS.

LETTER		PAGE
I.	"THE MOB OF CONSUMERS:" THE AMERICAN FARMERS AND THEIR EXPORTS................	3
II.	FARMERS AND OTHER WORKERS: THE TAX ON SALT...	6
III.	WHAT IT COSTS THE FARMER FOR LUMBER.......	1
IV.	WHAT IT COSTS THE FARMER FOR WINDOW-GLASS AND PLASTER.................................	16
V.	WHAT IT COSTS THE FARMER FOR OIL-CLOTH AND CARPETS..................................	22
VI.	WHAT IT COSTS THE FARMER FOR CROCKERY, GLASSWARE, AND COOKING UTENSILS..........	28
VII.	WHAT IT COSTS THE FARMER FOR BAGGING......	34
VIII.	WHAT IT COSTS TO INDULGE IN THE GREAT LUXURY OF HOSIERY............................	39
IX.	WHAT IT COSTS TO INDULGE IN THE GREAT LUXURY OF COTTON CLOTH.....................	45
X.	AN EXAMINATION OF THE TAX ON SPOOL THREAD.	50
XI.	THE EFFECT OF THE DUTY ON SILK GOODS......	53

Contents.

LETTER		PAGE
XII.	FEMALE LABOR ON FARMS AND IN FACTORIES	60
XIII.	THE TAXES ON COTTON-TIES	65
XIV.	TO MY FRIENDS, THE FARMERS OF THE UNITED STATES: A SUMMING UP	68
XV.	THAT AWFUL SURPLUS	73
XVI.	OUR VILLAINOUS TARIFF	81
XVII.	THE PINNACLE OF THE TARIFF SWINDLE	87
XVIII.	AS TO LUXURIES AND NECESSITIES	89
XIX.	A NATION MADE HAPPY AND RICH BY HIGH TAXATION	94
XX.	WAR TAXES IN TIME OF PEACE	97
XXI.	THE CHAMPION TARIFF SWINDLE OF THE WORLD	99

PREFACE.

These letters are selected from the much larger number printed during the last two years in the New York *Times* and *Evening Post*, and have been rearranged and modified to give a more continuous view of our iniquitous tariff system, with especial reference to the burden upon our farmers. The letters were based on topics of the day, and in rearranging them logically are thrown somewhat out of their chronological order; an endeavor has been made, however, to omit references to merely ephemeral matters, and it is hoped that in this shape the work may have more than a merely temporary value.   J. S. Moore.

LETTER I.

"THE MOB OF CONSUMERS:" THE AMERICAN FARMERS AND THEIR EXPORTS.

THIRTY years ago Mr. John Bright, that sturdy Macduff to the protection Macbeth of the world, laid down the axiom that protection is a combination of "knavery and folly," an epithet that has now become immortal. A short time ago Mr. Bright still more forcibly exemplified the protection system as an organized army against the consumers, who are simply a mob. Never was an expression more trite or more true. The organized armies are chiefly kept up by the autocrats to keep the populations of those unhappy countries (who are in their eyes only a mob) in order and duly oppressed. Our own tariff system is an organized legal tyranny to oppress sixty millions of consumers. Yes, consumers are but a mob, and an ignorant mob at that; or else how would it be possible to endure the most vexatious exactions for years without an earnest effort to break up the organized army of protection?

Of all the poor, deluded, tariff-ridden mob of consumers no one makes a more pitiable show than does the farmer of the United States. To him organized protection is the daughter of the horse-leech, and he has to " give," " give," " give " from the moment he gets up in the morning, when he washes his hands with taxed soap, until he goes to bed with a taxed " nightcap," if he still wears one. From the cradle to the grave he is taxed without any mitigation. To him protection of home industry is simply to give and not to receive. What a swindle it is, for instance, to put a duty on wheat, when all the wheat we imported during 1886 was 380,540 bushels, while our exports of wheat during the same year were 57,759,209 bushels, besides 8,000,000 barrels of flour. The farmer, serf to the organized army of protection, is not benefited one cent by the protection of wheat. He gets in New York the price, less freight and charges, that the wheat sells for in London. For instance, I see that American wheat on the 29th of April was selling in London for 7s. 2d. per 100 pounds, which is as near as possible $1.03 for a bushel of 60 pounds. The price in New York was 93 cents, leaving 10 cents a bushel for freight and charges and profit to London. Now, as the farmer in the United States only gets the London price less charges for his wheat, which is 93 cents net, let me show how much granulated sugar 10 bushels of wheat at 93 cents net will buy in London, and how much it will buy in New York. The price for granulated sugar in London is 16s. per hundredweight, or for 112 pounds, which is as near as possible 3½ cents per pound. The price for the same kind of sugar in New York in wholesale is 5¾ cents per pound.

With these facts before us we find that 10 bushels of wheat at 93 cents in New York, or $9.30, will buy a little less than 162 pounds of granulated sugar at 5¾ cents per pound. The same 10 bushels of wheat at 93 cents net in London, or $9.30, will buy as near as possible 265½ pounds of granulated sugar in London at 3½ cents per pound. In other words, when the American farmer wants to turn 10 bushels of his wheat into sugar in London he gets 265½ pounds, and if he wants to do the same thing in New York he gets only 162 pounds, or 103½ pounds less.

In 1886 we exported 63,656,433 bushels of Indian corn. The price of corn in London is at present 20s. per 480 pounds, or, as near as possible, 1 cent per pound. Now, a bushel of corn weighing 50 pounds is selling for 47½ cents in New York. That 2½ cents that it is selling more for in London is for freight, etc. Anyhow, the farmer does not get any more for his corn in New York than in London, less expenses. Well, then, 10 bushels of corn in New York at 47½ cents, or $4.75 if converted into granulated sugar at 5¾ cents per pound, will buy, as near as possible, 825⅝ pounds of sugar in New York.

On the other hand, 10 bushels of corn, the net price of which, less charges, is $4.75 in London, if converted into granulated sugar at 3½ cents per pound, will buy a fraction over 135⅝ pounds, or 53 pounds more in London than in New York.

With these little statistics as a mere beginning I will leave my fellow-mobsmen consumers, namely, the farmers, to reflect on the army organization of protection. But I promise to show the tyranny and swindle up *ad infinitum*.

MAY 3, 1887.

LETTER II.

FARMERS AND OTHER WORKERS: THE TAX ON SALT.

THE census of 1880 gives the following official and interesting returns of the number of people occupied in pursuing a gainful occupation. The total number was 17,392,099. The division was as follows:

Engaged in agriculture	7,670,493
Professional and personal service	4,074,238
Trade and transportation	1,810,256
Manufacturing, mechanical and mining	3,837,112
Total	17,392,099

But the actual number employed in manufacturing was:

Males about 16 years old	2,025,335
Females above 15 years old	531,639
Children	181,921
Total	2,738,895

Now these 2,738,895 are the actual army, officered and marshalled by protection, to whom the whole population has to pay tribute in the shape of tariff tax. When we look at this thing calmly we may well subscribe to the sagacity of Mr. Bright, who, in one sentence, defines the whole situation by describing the protectionists as an organized army, and the bulk of the population as a " mob " of consumers.

In the first place it will be seen that there are six times more people engaged in all other business, and nearly three times more in farming, than in manufacturing. Yet statesmen and orators will coolly cry themselves hoarse by pointing out that the existence and welfare of the whole 60,000,000 of our population rests upon high taxation in order that higher wages can be paid to these 2,738,000 mechanics. Of course, as protection is a mixture of knavery and ignorance, those who are ignorant of the fact cannot point out that a day's or a week's wages will buy more of anything except bread and meat in Europe than in the United States. And those who do know it and omit to state it are the other set. But what would this country be without its farmers? Only see what is going on around us. The 2,700,000 people employed in mechanical industries have for several years past been discontented, more or less turbulent, dissatisfied with employers. There are strikes almost every week; hundreds of thousands are in want and misery; full of grievances, whether real or not, yet grievances. And all this in the very teeth of protection, which the apostles of the protection Baal hold up as the only remedy for all evils. True, not only hundreds but thousands of millions of dollars have been gained by perhaps a hundred corporations or single individuals. The tariff on steel rails and steel, according to the uncontradicted statement of the Hon. William L. Scott, of Erie, Pa., has made the income of one single individual in Pennsylvania $5000 a day. There are now, I believe, only 11 steel-rail corporations, who by dint of a duty of $17 a ton on rails will pocket at least $20,000,000 bonus on home-made rails during the year 1887. There are hundreds of others of such monopolies whose bonus income by the grace of the tariff amounts to hundreds of millions of dollars. Still, what good is that to the community at large? Strikes, discontents, vexations, and disturbances go on all the same, and that is the result of protection.

Now turn to the farmers. There are 7,670,000 human beings actually employed and at work in the pursuit of farming. Is there, can there be, a more orderly or more worthy, a more law-abiding and peace-loving population on the globe? In 1880 there were 4,008,907 separate farms of all kinds and sizes held in the United States. The value of these farms, without any movables on them, was $10,197,096,776, or say, in round sum, nearly $10,200,000,000, while the whole capital invested in manufacturing in 1880 was $2,790,272,606, or not quite 28 per cent. as compared with the value of the farms alone without the cattle. Yet this mighty, industrious, hard-working, and without intending to be at all sentimental, blessed population is nothing better than a mob of consumers, subject to an organized army of protectionists.

Let me show the farmer in this communication what tax he pays on that awful luxury to man and beast known as salt. In 1886 we imported $1,493,397 worth of foreign salt. Of this amount $126,899, being salt used by curers of fish, did not pay any duty, but came in either free or the duty was remitted. The tariff laws are so beautifully arranged that it treats some as loving children and others as step-children. The fishermen being the actual children of Eastern tariff-makers get their salt for curing fish free of duty. But the farmers, being stepchildren, have to pay 83 per cent. duty on bulk salt and 39 per cent. on salt in bags if they want to use salt in their farm-houses. The Treasury, groaning under a surplus of $100,000,000, saw fit to collect a duty in 1886 of $706,324.34 on foreign salt. The home production is valued at about $5,000,000. This being enhanced at least by dint of the tariff, say, $2,000,000, it therefore follows that the country pays a tax of some $2,700,000 for the luxury of using salt, more than half of which is paid by the farmers. I pass over the wrong and outrage that the farmer should pay a tax of 12 cents per 100 pounds on salt in bags, or 8 cents per 100 pounds in bulk, when the fishermen of Gloucester get their bulk salt free for curing fish, but come rather back to the stern, dry fact of a tax on salt at all. I believe India and the United States are now the only chief countries that have a salt tax. In India the salt tax is very little; but the population of British India being 250,000,000, this very infinitesimal tax aggregates to a very large sum, and is, in fact, the only sure tax that the Treasury can collect to make the bulk of the people contribute to the expense of government. But what shall we say to a great country which is literally embarrassed by a surplus revenue of more than $100,000,000 annually, and has been so for at least 10 years past, and therefore does not need this revenue, to tax the whole population some $3,000,000 annually in order to pay a bonus to the home-made salt establishments? I am not a farmer, but I know that good farming requires salt besides what is used in the house. Salt is used for salting hay. It is used for cattle, and, of course, for dairy purposes.

In 1880 there was employed in the making of salt in the United States 4125 males above 16 years old, 20 women, and 144 children. Yet to this organized army of 4289, men, women, and children some 60,000,000 of the population have become a mob of consumers, and pay $3,000,000 annual tax. And to add insult to injury, this important swindle, this legal tariff robbery, is actually called a blessing. Let the farmers of this country reflect upon this. Let them feel ashamed of the paucity of their understanding, as it is really difficult to see how millions of men with common understanding can submit to become a mob of consumers and be fleeced by an organized army of protectionists.

But my hitherto attention to the farmers is only begun. I intend to show them how the tariff swindles them out of their hard-earned substance in hundreds of different necessaries of life they have to use.

MAY 12, 1887.

LETTER III.

WHAT IT COSTS THE FARMER FOR LUMBER.

IN my last two letters on the subject of how farmers are taxed I have somehow anticipated the regular order of my design. I have shown our dear good-natured American "Hodges" how they are oppressed by the sugar duty and swindled on the salt tax. These two articles are, of course, used in the house. I ought to have begun the exposé of the great tariff robbery on the materials the farm-house, barns, and stables are built of. I will make good this omission to-day. Of course we all know that timber and lumber is the material from which farm habitations, barns, and stables are built.

Well, then, the tax on every 1000 feet of lumber not planed or finished is $2. Of this class of lumber we imported in 1886 $5,243,736 worth, and the Treasury received $867,848 duty on it. That this lumber is enhanced $2 a thousand feet to the consumer, whether imported or produced in Maine or Michigan, is as clear as the sun at noonday. Now our friend Hodge, in Kansas or Iowa or Nebraska, having lived in a shanty for seven years, raising wheat or corn, and receiving for his product (as I have clearly proved over and over again) the price prevailing in London and Paris, who, therefore is not beholden in any way or manner to an enhancement of prices by the mock duty that tariff tricksters have put on foreign wheat and corn, has saved enough money, laid by during, say, seven years, stinting himself in all sorts of manner, to build what he considers a nice house for Mrs. Hodge and the children. Of course, in doing so, the chief material is lumber; but in steps the tariff and says *pay toll* of $2 on every thousand feet of lumber you use on the premises. If Farmer Hodge were not a *hodge*, but a reasonable, intelligent American citizen, he would first of all know that he does pay a tax of $2 on a thousand feet of lumber, and I honestly believe there are not 10 per cent. of the 30,000,000 of the Hodge family, comprising men, women, and children, who know the fact and understand it. Suppose, now, the intelligent Hodge who does understand this fact were to ask the following question : Why should I pay $2 a thousand feet on lumber when the Treasury is overflowing with an annual surplus of $100,000,000 ? The answer he would get would be as follows : You see, friend Hodge, there are the State of Maine and the State of Michigan, where we grow our own native aristocratic timber ; and that our timber is aristocratic is perfectly demonstrated by its diminutive and puny size and calibre, just the same as the true aristocratic descendants of a long line of blue-blooded ancestors of France and Spain are known by their puny and diminutive statures. Well, then, we must first of all protect our aristocratic timber and lumber, because it cannot compete with the pauper lumber of Canada, which has not a drop of aristocratic blue blood in it.

Then again, friend Hodge, if you don't pay $2 tax on a thousand feet of lumber, Maine, Michigan, and other timber-producing States will be deprived of at least $25,000,000, or perhaps $30,000,000, of bonus annually. And lastly, brother Hodge, of Kansas and Nebraska, if you don't pay a tax on timber we in Michigan and Maine will not eat any of your wheat, and then you will be a pauper farmer. Poor Hodge may scratch his head trying to find something in it to answer these forcible arguments. But as he is not expected to be a statistician let me help him out.

Of course the aristocratic home-timber dodge against the pauper-labor timber of Canada is a pleasantry not worth noticing. The plea for not being deprived of $25,000,000 bonus is intelligent on account of self-interest inherent in mankind. But the plea that the farmers' wheat is benefited by the consumers of the timber regions is simply a big *lie*. And here I'll prove it. The great bulk of the lumber produced in the United States was as follows, according to the census of 1880 :

Michigan	$52,449,928	Ohio	$13,864,460
Pennsylvania	22,457,359	Maine	7,933,806
Indiana	14,260,830	Iowa	6,185,628
New York	14,356,910	Missouri	5,265,617
Wisconsin	17,952,347	Illinois	5,063,037

These are the States chiefly interested. Now, there are only three States in the above list that do not export both wheat and corn, and they are Maine, New York, and Pennsylvania. In 1880 the State of New York raised 11,587,766 bushels of wheat, and needed about 12,000,000 bushels in addition from all the other States. Besides this New York produces over $14,000,000 of lumber annually. Pennsylvania raised 19,462,405 bushels of wheat, and did not need any wheat raised outside her own State. The State of Maine consumes about 3,500,000 bushels of wheat and raised 665,714 bushels. That is, this State buys about 3,000,000 bushels of wheat outside her own State. Altogether, say, New York and Maine need 15,000,000 bushels of wheat over and above what is raised in these States. Yet it is impudently and maliciously asserted that these 15,000,000 bushels of wheat consumption will affect the total wheat production of the country, when we raise about 500,000,000 bushels and export more than 100,000,000 bushels of wheat, including wheat flour. And let it be fully understood, this argument of consumption of cereals is made by the organized army of protection in everything that the farmer uses, from wood-screws to horseshoe nails. But let us come back to Mr. Hodge's house. Having paid a tax of $2 a thousand feet on lumber, he pays a tax of 30 per cent. on the screws he uses, 40 per cent. on the nails, and, of course, he pays a tax on the iron hinges and door-locks.

Now, we certainly must put a couple of coats of paint on friend Hodge's house. The tax or duty on white lead is 3 cents a pound. Although, I am bound to state, at the present moment there is a nice little cut-throat competition going on between the far West and the East in the production and price of white lead, which for the time being has reduced the price. But the duty is 3 cents a pound, and in 1886 we even at that duty imported 755,103 pounds of white lead. Should Mr. Hodge desire to put a slate roof on his house he has to pay 25 per cent. duty on the slates.

Having so far raised the house for the Hodge family and painted it, I shall in my next communication put windows in his house, plaster it, and otherwise finish it. For the present Mr. Hodge may reflect on the taxes he has to pay on the luxury of using lumber, nails, wood-screws, paint, and slates.

MAY 18, 1887.

LETTER IV.

WHAT IT COSTS THE FARMER FOR WINDOW-GLASS AND PLASTER.

In my last communication I promised to provide Mr. Hodge's new house with windows. It will be recollected that I already showed him the tax he has to pay on lumber, paint, screws, nails, hinges, and slate. I will try to astonish him—that is if there is such a thing as astonishment left in Mr. Hodge—by showing how he is swindled and robbed by the tariff in using window-glass and Paris plaster for his new house. Let me give a little history of window-glass. This infant industry, using the very graphic language of Mr. Butterworth, of Ohio, wears a full-size overcoat and No. 10 shoes. In 1880, or seven years ago, the production of window-glass was valued at $5,047,313. The quantity produced was 1,864,000 boxes of 50 square feet each. The total wages paid to produce this special kind of glass was $2,139,500, and the total number of hands employed was 3735 men, 1 woman, and 134 children. The average duty on window-glass in 1886 was 86 13 per cent., and the Treasury actually collected a revenue of $1,174,340.62 on common window-glass, and to the home manufacturers a further bonus, taking into the account the increase of production since 1880, of no less than $40,000,000 was paid. Altogether it costs about $50,000,000 tax annually to use the commonest kind of window-glass. To tax a man's daylight in his habitation is above all other taxes a refined cruelty. From the time of Pitt to Sir Robert Peel England had a window-glass excise tax. But even then there was a discrimination. For instance, up to a certain size the glass was not taxed. But when people chose to indulge in larger panes of glass for their windows they had to pay a tax. Hence we found, up to 1846, in England millions of houses with very small-sized panes of glass in the windows. So obnoxious was this tax that Lord Byron facetiously said that there was a great excuse for Englishmen damning their eyes because the Government set them the example of damming the daylight in their houses. But England had at least the excuse of getting all the tax she could in order to pay the interest on her debt of £900,000,000. Then, again, every shilling of this tax was paid into the exchequer. Now, look at the American window-glass tax. The Treasury is overflowing with $100,000,000 surplus. The tax is not needed. Yet, over $5,000,000 is squeezed out of the window-tax in order to pay high wages to 3735 men, 1 woman, and 134 children.

Now, let me analyze these aristocratic wages: I stated that in 1880 the total wages were $2,139,500. Suppose we divide the average thus: 3735 men averaging $11 a week is $2,136,420, leaving some $3000 wages for the 134 children and 1 woman. In other words, considering that glass-making is a most laborious, unwholesome, disgustingly hot, and very trying handicraft, $11 a week is by no means very aristocratic wages, especially as a man's life in that kind of work is short. Yet with these facts before us the country is taxed over 86 per cent. on this indispensable necessary of life. But on whom does this tax fall heaviest? Why, on the poor, good-natured Hodges. There are now, in 1887, at least 5,000,000 separate farm-houses. (There were seven years ago over 4,000,000.) The breakage of glass in these houses, and above all the glass used in new ones built, pay the bulk of this task, because they all use that common kind of windowglass. Well, then, with this little preface, let me get back to my friend Hodge's new house. Suppose my rural friend supplies his house with $50 worth of glass. Of course I make these estimates purposely moderate, as I address myself to the hard-working, independent, but not rich, citizens. In order to pay $50 for the window-glass, Mr. Hodge has to sell, say, in round numbers, 60 bushels of wheat or 125 bushels of corn. To him this product is as much an income as the income of a coupon is to the millionaire who has bonds. The tariff does not favor him 1 cent on either corn or wheat. More than 80 per cent. of this window-glass is produced in Pennsylvania, Illinois, Indiana, Ohio, Maryland, and Michigan, States that need not go outside for corn or wheat, but most of them are exporters of both. Therefore the $50 Mr. Hodge has to spend for the windows of his house being derived from the products of his farm, and having the same value in England, France, and Germany, loses all at once the purchasing power when he wants to buy home-made or imported window-glass. That is to say, if there were no duty on window-glass, Mr. Hodge would buy for $27 the quantity of glass for which he has now to pay $50. In other words, he is taxed and swindled out of $23 for the great luxury of being allowed to have windows in his house.

But our rural friend Hodge does not know, of course, that in large cities, where one-hundred-thousand-dollar houses are built, the dwellers therein would no more think of using common green cylinder glass for their windows than they would use the Russian black bread. These rich and happy people don't pay 86 per cent. for their window-glass; they use fine plate-glass. Such plate-glass, even if it is of the size of 24 by 30 inches, only pays 27 per cent. duty.

There are two classes that do not feel the hardships of an American tariff. First, the real pauper; he of course does not pay any tax. The next class is the millionaire or rich man who indulges in luxuries. It is the middle class, the hard-working " Hodges," the wage-earning mechanics and artisans; they are the bone and sinew; they are the multitude, and they have to pay to the organized army of the protection oligarchy an oppressive tax on every necessary of life, and are even derided, scolded, and cursed if they look in any other way on this legal robbery than a national blessing. But let me get through with this villainous outrage. Mr. Hodge's common green glass windows are in his house. Tax, 86.13 per cent. Now it certainly is conducive to appearance and more so to health to have the rooms plastered. To plaster rooms we must use whiting or Paris white. The duty on this great luxury is ½ cent a pound, equal in 1886 to 89.38 per cent. ad valorem. The reason for this tax is probably that American whiting or Paris white is only an infant and does not yet wear an overcoat and No. 10 shoes. The Treasury got $7000 duty in 1885 and $4495 in 1886. But the Hodges paid no doubt hundreds of thousands of dollars to the infant home-made Paris white monopolists. The following interesting news appeared in a leading New York protectionist paper:

A New Yorker who is much interested in the tariff is Le Grand B. Cannon. He is heavily engaged in coal and iron enterprises, especially in the Delaware and Hudson Canal Company Railroad and mines. Probably few men in New York do more executive work in a day than Mr. Cannon. Among his numerous other trusts he is a member of the American Protective Tariff League. When met up-town the other day he said: "Our League will accomplish some great work next year. We have started among other things a list of 1000 names of subscribers who propose to pay $100 a year toward the support of the League as an educational organization. We have already such a start on this list that we are certain of accomplishing the desired result. We will be able to make a great demonstration of the strength and force of the organized protective tariff interests when the Congressional elections come off next year. We propose to put a series of interrogations to every man that is nominated. If he refuses to answer them or cannot answer satisfactorily we propose to lay him out. Party politics will not enter into the question at all. It will simply be a question whether the man is a friend of protective tariff or not."

Let the farmers, the hard-working Hodges of the country, read the above carefully. First, there is to be expended $100,000 annually for an "*Educational Organization.*" This expression is a vast improvement on Mr. C. P. Huntington's "*Explanation Organization.*" Then if a candidate for Congress cannot answer a series of interrogations properly he will be "laid out." That is to say, if the candidate for Congress is asked: Will you vote for a reduction on the farmer's taxes, which now are:

>Duty on lumber, $2 per 1000 feet.
>Duty on screws, 30 per cent.
>Duty on nails, 40 per cent.
>Duty on hinges, 40 per cent.
>Duty on paint, if white lead, 3 cents a pound.
>Duty on slates, 25 per cent.
>Duty on common window-glass, 86.13 per cent.
>Duty on plastering, 89.38 per cent.

And the unfortunate candidate hesitatingly should answer : "Well, these high taxes on the hard-working farmers ought to be reduced," he will be "laid out." The $100,000 educational organization will not allow itself to be trifled with. Are the 30,000,000 or 35,000,000 farmers of the country so purblind as not to see the bondage in its true light? At present I have only shown a mere beginning of the tax robbery to which they are now slaves. When I get through with the whole catalogue of iniquities the $100,000 education organization fund will hardly be a drop in the bucket. I would advise this organization to procure a few thousand poisonous salamanders to poison the truth. A time is coming, particularly in tariff reform, when the use of money in " laying out " candidates will recoil on the bloated protectionist oligarchy and slay them with their own weapon.

MAY 26, 1887.

LETTER V.

WHAT IT COSTS THE FARMER FOR OIL-CLOTH AND CARPETS.

NOTHING is more plausible for the ignorant or the wily protection advocates than the stereotyped legend, " Tax luxuries high and put a moderate tax on common necessaries." Some time ago I showed in the deadly parallel column that in the American tariff system it is just the reverse. For instance, a rich man who can afford to drink a bottle of dear still wine costing $3 or $4 will only pay a tax of at most 15 per cent., and on champagne the average duty in 1886 was 52 per cent. But the tax on castor-oil was in 1886 no less than 189.28 per cent. Perhaps I am wrong after all. There may be a greater luxury in castor-oil than in a bottle of champagne or Château Yquem. The latter may bring pain. The former in general relieves it. I am therefore puzzled how to class a luxury or a necessity.

Our friend the farmer who builds a new house (which protectionists may, first of all, consider a luxury) may be desirous to put down some floor oil-cloth, a drugget carpet, and even a tapestry carpet. Should the American farmer entertain such a luxurious ambition as using oil-cloth, he should certainly be made aware that this free, rich, and great country imposes a severe tax on such extravagance, not because there is a heavy interest on the national debt to pay, nor indeed is the tax wanted at all, as the country is actually cursed with a surplus of $100,000,000 annually, but simply for the best of all reasons, that there were in 1880 the following hands employed in the floor oil-cloth business, namely, 1690 men, 5 women, and 40 children, and these received a total of $733,235 wages, which would give an average of about $8.25 a week to the men. Hence the duty on floor oil-cloth is 40 per cent. In 1880 the value of floor-cloth produced at home was $4,721,066. I dare say it is now at least $6,000,000. The enhanced tax paid on this home-made product is at least $1,500,000, and we collected in 1886 a duty of $110,347, and the account stands thus :

Paid in 1886 to home-made floor-cloth tax $1,500,000
Paid to the Treasury duty on floor-cloth.   110,347

Total........................ $1,610,347

With these little statistics before us, I beg to call the farmer's attention who has built a new house, that if he wants to buy $50 worth of oil-cloth the tax thereon is about $14; or, in other words, he has to raise 17½ bushels of wheat at 80 cents a bushel to pay an "*extra tax*" on $50 worth of oil-cloth. The value of a yard of floor oil-cloth abroad in 1886 was 63 cents.

The next great luxury that the farmer's wife may desire for her rooms is common drugget. Well, this luxurious article costs abroad 36½ cents a square yard, and the duty thereon is 15 cents per square yard, and in addition thereto 30 per cent. ad valorem, or say altogether 71.40 per cent. Should Mrs. Hodge indulge in this great luxury and need, say, 109 yards only, she will have to pay an extra tax, as near as possible, of $26. And her worthy husband will have to raise 25½ bushels of wheat at 80 cents per bushel, *not* to pay for any extra value in the carpet, but simply for the "tax." There is at least one room left which will be furnished with that showy and lively looking carpet known as tapestry Brussels. The duty on this goods was, in 1886, 59.36 per cent. This carpet costs 68 cents a square yard abroad. Should the farm-house parlor need 40 square yards of carpet, the farmer will pay an extra tax of $16.34 and raise 20 bushels of wheat to pay the extra tax. Thus, then, furnishing his house with the cheapest kind of floor-cloth and carpeting, it costs him :

On floor cloth tax... $14.00 | On tapestry........ 16.34
On druggets tax .... 26.00 |
    Total....................................$56.34

This may in some measure look small. But suppose there are of the 5,000,000 separate farms now in the country only 2 per cent. newly built and rebuilt, that would be 100,000 houses. If each should pay this outrageous swindling tax it would aggregate over $5,600,000. That is, this good, solid money is taken from the farmers without the least compensation to uphold the so-much-lauded American home system.

Before I conclude this letter it is once more necessary for me (perhaps for the hundredth time) to state that nothing is more misleading than the protectionists' irrepressible assertations that goods, although highly protected, are sold here as cheap as abroad. I was especially amused when this assertion was pointed out to me a few days ago in a private letter as to tapestry carpets. Well, then, let me demolish this supposition. There is tapestry carpet, home-made, sold all the way from 45 cents to perhaps $1.25 a yard; all depends on quality.

The kind of tapestry carpet sold here for, say

50 cents a running yard, cannot be imported, as it is entirely prohibited. Such a carpet no doubt sells in England for about 1s. 3d. a running yard, or 30 cents. The lowest duty on tapestry carpet is 20 cents a square yard, and in addition 30 per cent. ad valorem. Hence, such a carpet is entirely prohibited. The lowest price tapestry carpet that can be imported costs in England about 68 cents a square yard, and the duty thereon is 59.36 per cent. In 1886 we imported 186,356 square yards of this carpet and paid a duty of $75,351 on it, which clearly proves that the consumers of tapestry carpet of a better class, such which costs 68 cents abroad, whether imported or home-made, has to pay 59.36 per cent. This I hope is clear enough for everybody to understand. That the full pound of flesh duty on nearly all carpets except perhaps the lowest price goods, which is, as shown, prohibited, is taken by our home manufacturers is demonstrated and proved by statistical facts, namely, in 1886 we imported $1,329,340 worth of carpets of all sorts and collected a duty of $659,874 on it at the average rate of 49.64 per cent.

Can any one in his sober senses believe that importers actually paid this $659,874 duty simply for the benefit of the Treasury? Or that English importers paid this duty? The fact is, in 1886 the carpet manufacturers of the United States paid a duty of $2,198,149 on foreign imported carpet wool. This fact alone must convince unbiassed minds that all our home-made carpets are bound to be higher in price. Free wool and free jute and a duty of 25, or even 30 per cent. on manufactured carpets will relieve both the manufacturer and the taxpayer.

Now I wish my much-swindled and oppressed taxpaying friends fully to understand that if I had it in my sole power to take off the whole tax or duty on oil floor-cloth, druggets, or carpets, and make them free of duty, I would certainly *not* do it all at once. I do not believe in a policy that goes from one extreme to the other, but with free carpet, wool, free jute, and free oil there is no necessity of a greater duty than 20 per cent. on the above articles, which would certainly not destroy the home industry, but would rather give our manufacturers a chance to export carpets and floor-cloth, and would relieve the consumers of these products of more than half the tax. But there is a cursed protection oligarchy astir that will not listen to reason. This wicked clique knows full well that protection is doomed, as was the worship of Moloch and Baal. But every year of respite, though it is a gallows respite, puts hundreds of millions of dollars, taken annually from the pockets of the multitude, into the pockets of the few thousand monopolists and corporations. And as long as that can be made to last, every effort will be made to keep it up. How Mr. Morrison, of Illinois, was disposed of by the tin-plate and cotton-ties protectionists of Pennsylvania is but too well known. How Mr. Randall, a so-called Democrat, was kept in Congress by the forbearance of a Republican protection district is a matter of history. And now we have in New York a little club known as the " Educational Organization." Capital, $100,000. Object of the organization, " *To lay unsatisfactory candidates out* " who refuse to keep up the present tariff system.

LETTER VI.

WHAT IT COSTS THE FARMER FOR CROCKERY, GLASSWARE, AND COOKING UTENSILS.

SENATOR SHERMAN, ex-Secretary of the Treasury, and for twelve years a Presidential-sick candidate, has told the people of this country in general and his hearers in Springfield, Ill., in particular, that our protective tariff is so justly and scientifically adjusted that, with the exception of the duty collected on sugar, which he benevolently considers a necessity, nearly all other duties are collected from articles of luxury mainly consumed by the rich. Such a statement would have been inexcusable almost, if it came from an ignorant backwoods stump speaker, but coming, as it did, from a Senator who has been many years Chairman of the Senate Finance Committee and ex-Secretary of the Treasury, it was worse than a wilful misstatement or political crime. It was simply a blunder. One is at a loss to understand how such a man could deliberately commit such an unheard-of folly. There may, however, have been an incident just fresh on the political tapis which compelled the Ohio statesman to commit this blunder, namely: An Industrial Protective League has been started in New York, whose object is, first of all, to raise a little revenue of $100,000 to be spent annually to educate the dull and the pervert, and second, should the dull and pervert who may happen to be candidates for Congress, and, of course, for the Presidential office, refuse to be educated, or not be up to the mark, they must be "laid out." Now, if there is a nightmare or any other shocking event which the Ohio statesman dreads more than anything else it is the fear of being "laid out" in the nomination as President in 1888. However, I will show to-day how the tariff affects the farmer on some articles which unsophisticated, plain, practical people would class as necessaries, but which in Senator Sherman's tariff definitions are luxuries.

In furnishing his new house, which the American farmer may build in the West, far West, or anywhere else, it is certainly necessary that he should have crockery and glassware. In the first place the question arises, Are crockery and glassware luxuries? I must admit that there are countries where crockery or chinaware and glass are luxuries. For instance, perhaps 80 per cent. of the Russian population, or nearly all the Laplanders, use wooden utensils, out of which they eat their food or drink water and "wudka." As the object of a protective tariff is to restrict commerce and intercourse, and the result even thus far, after 25 years of the existence of the American tariff, has tended to narrow the immense wealth of the country into the possession of a limited number of cunning millionaires, it is, of course, only a question of time when this great republic will be divided into two classes—the great feudal millionaires and the working serfs. Don't let my readers rashly think that this assertion is merely a vain supposition. When the proud multitude become poor and needy it is then that the wealth of the few becomes powerful. Wealth and extreme wealth in the hands of the few has proved this in every country during the last 2000 years. Just see the assumption of this in the very fact of this New York Protective League. As a beginning $100,000 will be spent annually in educating to keep up monopolies, and in "laying out" those who may have a will of their own and desire a Congressional position. But I digress. All I want to show is that as we are surely getting poorer—I mean the great multitude—a time may not be far off when crockery and chinaware will be considered a luxury, and we may go back to the use of wooden utensils. But as the farmer is still independent and believes, God help him! that he is not very outrageously taxed, I will merely show him what it costs him for the luxury of using plates, cups and saucers, and glassware.

The duty on "china, porcelain, parian, and bisque ware, plain white, and not ornamented or decorated in any manner," is 55 per cent Now, let the farmer and, for that matter, any other "tariff serf" remember this duty is for plain, unornamented, and unpainted crockery. On painted and decorated it is 60 per cent. Is the farmer aware what 55 per cent. means? It is, of course, more than one-third the value of the goods. Or, in other words, if he buys $15 worth of crockery he pays a tax of about $5.25 to somebody, either to the Government or home manufacturer. The total consumption of crockery and chinaware is about as near as possible:

Home-made at present...............	$10,000,000
Imported in 1886...................	4,992,214
The duty on the imported was........	2,829,535
Total........................	$17,821,749

The average duty was 57.80 per cent. At the very lowest calculation the country paid a tax of about $6,000,000 in 1886 for the priviledge of using crockery. And now let me show what this mighty home industry really is. In 1880, according to the census, the whole capital invested in the manufacture of stone, crockery, and china ware was $6,380,000. (Perhaps much of this assumed capital was watered.) But let us say there really is $6,-

000,000 invested in this industry. It would follow that the consumers of crockery are annually taxed as much as will pay for all the capital invested. In 1880 the hands employed were :

    Men........................ 7,205
    Women..................... 948
    Children................... 1341

The total wages paid them were $3,279,535. Now, suppose the wages are now $4,000,000. Then it follows that the country is taxed not only the total wages paid, but $2,000,000 in addition (that is, $6,000,000), to enable the aristocratic potteries of the United States to compete with the pauper potteries of Europe.

Now, there is another phase to this. Up to 1883 the duty on crockery was respectively 40, 45, and 50 per cent. This heavy duty was raised by the Tariff Commission in 1883—a commission specially created to reduce duties —20 per cent. in average, to 55 and 60 per cent. In other words crockery that paid in 1882 40 per cent. duty now pays 55 per cent., and china that paid 50 per cent. duty now pays 60 per cent. The average duty on earthenware in 1883, before the Tariff Commission bill came in force, was 43.10 per cent., and in 1886 it was 57.80 per cent. And yet any candidate for Congress who would dare to question this tariff swindle, this tariff robbery, will be " laid out " by the New York Protection Educational Club, " capital unlimited," annual revenue $100,000. Now, if there is any " laying out " to be done, why not lay out these facts and figures? Here is a chance. Why, in fact, not lay out all my figures and statements? My letters to the farmers are reprinted and noticed all over the land. Why not lay them out? The duty on glassware used in farm-houses and by the poorest people, who are not paupers, is 40 per cent. The better and higher priced is 45 per cent. The duty on table knives and forks is 35 per cent. The duty on hollow-ware, in which the farmers' breakfasts and dinners are cooked, if coated and glazed, is 45.37 per cent.

As it is my purpose to show the farmers in a practical shape and in detail the taxes they are oppressed with on account of our swindling tariff system, I shall give a detailed list as far as I have collected it. The tax monster is only in its babyhood now. But still it is as follows:

 Tax on lumber, $2 per 1000 feet.
 Tax on screws, 30 per cent.
 Tax on nails, 40 per cent.
 Tax on hinges, 40 per cent.
 Tax on paint, 3 cents a pound.
 Tax on slates, 25 per cent.
 Tax on common window-glass, 86.13 per cent.
 Tax on plastering, 89.38 per cent.
 Tax on oil-cloth, 40 per cent.
 Tax on druggets, 71.40 per cent.
 Tax on tapestry carpet, 59.36 per cent.
 Tax on crockery, 55 per cent.
 Tax on common glassware, 40 per cent.
 Tax on table knives and forks, 35 per cent.
 Tax on hollow ware, glazed, 45.37 per cent.

But the real outrageous taxes that the farmer has to pay have not been touched as yet.

All I can say to the farmers, and indeed to all the tax-ridden community, is that I intend to do this work thoroughly, and fully expose the leprosy of our tariff system before I get through.

JUNE 8, 1887.

LETTER VII.

WHAT IT COSTS THE FARMER FOR BAGGING.

I WOULD like to ask the farmers and planters of this country a simple question, and that is, *Whether they consider a grain bag or coarse hemp or jute cloth for baling cotton a luxury?*

Surely there can be but one answer to this question—that not only is it not a luxury, but a necessity, which is indispensable to farmers and planters. Without a grain bag the farmer could not carry his grain to market and to the mill. Without cotton baling the planter could not make his cotton crop available and marketable. It is as much a necessity to the now perhaps 20,000,000 people employed in agricultural pursuits as is the necessity of their own labor.

Now, suppose a paternal Government were to put a tax on actual farm-hands; that is, suppose the farmer would have to pay a tax of only $5 a year on every laborer he employs. What would be the political result? I leave the answer to the farmers. Yet the farmers and planters pay a heavy tax on grain bags and cotton balings without the least grumbling. Sweet is the result of ignorance. The cunning and scheming tariff oppressors always find their true and most potent ally in the ignorance and gullibility of the great masses. To use an expression of Dr. Goldsmith, "They ride the multitude as the groom rides his horse, simply because the groom is more cunning than the horse."

How strange and inconsistent are the ways in this world. When some 34 years ago I was for the first time in "Point de Galle," in Ceylon. I went, as a matter of course, to see the Buddhist temple, situated in the Sacred Grove some four miles from the town. The first thing that struck me was an immense plain masonry structure about 12 feet high, shaped exactly like a beehive, and looking for all the world like a beehive. The circumference was, as near as I can recollect, about that of the base of the Statue of Liberty. There are numerous small-sized holes about 6 feet high all around this masonry beehive for the faithful to deposit money in. These donations, the natives are told, are appropriated by Buddha himself. As the yellow-robed priests declare there is nothing of it in the beehive, yet it has been standing there for hundreds, perhaps thousands of years. Strange enough, I met an American missionary there with whom I had a conversation. He it was who pointed this swindle out to me. How little did I dream then that I would have to point out many thousand Buddhist beehives and swindles to his own countrymen and in his own free country! Yes! American protection is a veritable Buddhist beehive receptacle for the ignorant, tax-ridden millions to put their hard earnings in. And the few thousand boss protectionists are the yellow-robed priests, who most solemnly assert and try to prove that such exactions are for the vital interest of the whole people. And now I will show the farmers and planters how much they put in the protection Buddhist beehive on grain bags and cotton baling.

The duty on bagging composed wholly of jute, jute butts, gunnycloth, etc., and used for the purpose of baling cotton, is $1\frac{1}{2}$ and 2 cents, respectively, per pound, and is equal to 54 per cent. and 49 per cent., respectively. The duty on bags and bagging used for grain is plain 40 per cent. The Treasury collected in 1886 the following revenue :

On bags and bagging for grain........$470,725
On bagging for cotton...............   11,515

In 1880 the home-made bags and bagging amounted to $13,238,253. Which now, seven years later, no doubt is at least $16,000,000.

There is, of course, not the slightest doubt that on every grain bag used by the farmers the tax is 40 per cent., and on the baling used by the planters, for baling cotton, it is about 49 per cent. Now, let me seriously ask the farmers and planters, inasmuch as these coverings and bags are as essential to their industry as the hands they employ, why in the world should these prime necessities be taxed? First let us see what this tax amounts to. If there is $16,000,000 worth of this necessity used annually, and the enhancement by dint of the tariff is only say 40 per cent. on an average, it follows that the amount of money the planter and farmer is taxed every year is about $4,500,000.

Of course the prime and original curse of all tariff taxation is the folly and crime of taxing raw material; and in this aforesaid product the raw material is taxed as follows:

> Flax not hackled or dressed, $20 a ton.
> Flax tow, $10 a ton.
> Hemp, $25 a ton.
> Hemp tow, $10 a ton.
> Jute, 20 per cent.
> Jute butts, $5 per ton.
> Sisal grass, $15 per ton.

Who can possibly doubt, if we were to give our manufacturers this raw material free of duty, that we could thereby benefit both the manufacturers and consumers? I shall take every opportunity I have in reiterating that my advocacy is *not absolute free trade* in manufactured goods. I aim and have aimed for 20 years for simple tariff reform, and in this very article of bags and bagging I solemnly declare that if Congress were to give free jute, hemp, and flax to the manufacturers, that I would still advocate a duty of 20 per cent. on bags and bagging, not because I consider any tax on these necessaries just or equitable, but simply because I have a great economical objection to step from one extreme to the other. A time will come when even our own manufacturers will feel that they are able to cope with foreign competition without protection.

With these remarks, freely and honestly expressed without reserve, I am now pointing out the villainous robbery and oppression of our tariff system, and leave it to the good sense of the multitude to say if the exposés and strictures I make on our tariff system can be denied. Whether the maintenance of this system is not a national crime and outrage. And now let me show the total wages, and so-called aristocratic wages paid in America in 1880, a year of great prosperity and boom for manufacturing bagging and bags. In 1880 there were employed in the manufacturing of bagging of all kinds, and also bags, made of jute, hemp, and flax, 2505 men, 2129 women, and 817 children; total, 5451.

In the first place we are struck by the fact that in this industry there are only 376 more men than women employed, and there are 817 boys below 15 years of age employed. The total wages paid these 5451 hands was, in 1880, $1,603,785. This would give the average wages divided as follows:

2505 men at $7 a week...............	$911,820
2129 women at $5 a week............	573,540
817 boys at $3 a week..............	127,492
Total........	$1,612,852

The farmers and planters can therefore see that they are being taxed annually over $4,500,000 on bags and bagging, while the whole wages in this industry was only $1,600,000 in 1880, and certainly cannot be over $2,000,000 at the present time. Now, as there is a Protection Educational Company in New York, capital unlimited, annual revenue $100,000, object to educate and "lay out," would it not be as well to begin by laying my facts and figures out? Why not try and show, for instance, that the farmer gets paid for his bags when he sells the meal, or the cotton-planter gets the price of bagging paid him at the value of cotton? Come, gentlemen of the Laying Out Club, try your hands at this. Here is a chance I give you. Why don't you take it?

June 15, 1887.

LETTER VIII.

WHAT IT COSTS TO INDULGE IN THE GREAT LUXURY OF HOSIERY.

One would hardly believe that in an American climate, and especially to the Anglo-Saxon race, stockings for women and children and half hose for men are a luxury. Yet it must be a very important luxury, according to the definition of the veteran statesman, for many years Senator, Chairman of the Senate Finance Committee, ex-Secretary of the Treasury, and embryo candidate for the Presidential nomination, Mr. John Sherman. As it will be remembered that the ex-Secretary of the Treasury said in his Springfield speech that, with the exception of the duty on sugar, the rest of the revenue from customs is collected on articles of luxury, mainly used by the rich. Of course, this is a rich country. We are all rich; in fact, we must be all rich, because 60,000,000 of the population can afford to pay a duty of 40 per cent. on the luxury of wearing cotton hosiery and 60.61 per cent. on woollen and worsted hosiery. And, now, let me relate and expose in detail this swindle, this robbery, a tax of 40 per cent. on cotton and over 60 per cent. on woollen hosiery, and I feel sure that the Ohio statesman and Presidential candidate will only be too ready to contradict his hasty statement about luxuries, and he may even class hosiery with sugar. History relates that great Generals have won battles by judicious retreats, and it would be vain to search for a great statesman-General who is more consummate in the tactics of retreating than Senator Sherman.

In 1886 the United States Treasury collected a revenue of $2,312,337.91 on common cotton stockings and half hose at the rate of 40 per cent. Perhaps the agricultural population, who have paid most of this tax, may better understand the enormity of a 40 per cent. tax when we put it in a more lucid way :

Cost in Europe of cotton hosiery imported in 1886	$5,780,744 81
Duty thereon at 40 per cent	2,312,337 91
Total cost to the people	$8,093,182 72
The importation of woollen hosiery in 1886 was, cost abroad	$1,930,389 19
Duty at 60.61 per cent. collected by the Treasury	1,132,994 98
Total	$3,063,384 17

Of this, over $11,000,000 worth of foreign hosiery, the Treasury exacted over $3,446,000. This much all the 60,000,000 of people paid to the Treasury for the luxury of wearing hosiery brought here from abroad. And now let me show what the 60,000,000 tariff serfs paid to the feudal lords at home for the use of home-made hosiery. In 1880, the census year, the production of home-made hosiery was valued at $20,167,227. Assuming that the production has increased to $35,000,000 in 1886 (which is, of course, largely underestimated), and if we only estimate the enhancement on account of the tariff one-third of the value of the production, it would then follow that the consumers of hosiery, whether of cotton or wool, paid some $11,666,000 to the home manufacturers in 1886, and the tax account would stand thus:

Tax paid Government, 1886, on cotton hosiery.	$2,312,337
Tax paid Government, 1886, on woollen hosiery.	1,132,994
Tax paid to home manufacturers	11,666,000
Total tax paid on hosiery in 1886	$15,111,331

In 1880 the whole capital invested in the hosiery manufacture in the United States was $15,579,501. That is to say, the tax in 1886 was within $468,000 as much as the whole capital invested in 1880 in this industry. The wages and salaries of all kinds paid in this industry in 1880 was $6,701,475, and if the wages paid in 1886 should have risen to $8,000,000 it would follow that the tax paid by the people during 1886 was over $7,000,000 more than the whole wages paid. But when we come to analyze this hosiery trade in America we may well marvel at the impudent and lying assertions made by the protectionists about the superior wages and great comfort of the working classes protected by this piratical protective tariff.

I leave it to my fellow-citizens whether it would not be reasonable to expect of a home industry that has a clear bonus, as I have shown, of $11,666,000 a year, that workmen should in the main be employed who will support their wives and children; instead of which this industry employs nearly three times more women and children than men. Let me show from the census of 1880 how this industry was supplied. Total hands employed in 1880, 28,885, which were divided thus :

Men over 16 years old	7,517
Women over 15 years old	17,707
Children under 16 years old	3,661
Total	28,885

Or, in other words, there were 21,368 women and children employed to 7517 men. When the American feudal hosiery baron in this year of jubilee travels on the continent of Europe in a first-class railway carriage and sees in the fields women and children employed during the harvest he is sure to call his wife and daughters, dressed *en voyage* in " Worth's " latest, to the window and point out to them the misery and degradation of the people who live under a monarchy and have not to the full extent the blessings of an American protective tariff. That in his own hosiery factory in Pennsylvania, Rhode Island, or Massachusetts there are shut up, if he employs 100 hands, some sixty-odd women and children who have to work 10 hours a day does not, of course, enter his mind, That his factory in such susceptible climates as we have in the Northern States is a breeder and rapid developing consumption establishment for tender women and children he never gives a thought, and that these hard-working women and children in the fields of Germany have at least the advantage of working in the fresh air, and are therefore better off than the factory hands, he will, of course, not admit. But I leave it to my fellow-citizens to decide, and now let us divide the aristocratic wages paid in America to the hands employed in the manufacture of hosiery.

The total wages and salaries paid in 1880 were $6,701,475 to 28,005 hands. Suppose we say that the wages paid to,

7,517 men were $7 a week............. $2,736,188
17,707 women at $4 a week............   3,683,056
3,661 children at $2 a week...........   380,744

   Total........................ $6,799,988

Which would actually be some $98,000 more than was paid. Now, I leave it to all fair-minded men whether a whole people should tax itself over $15,000,000 annually by protecting the hosiery industry 40 and 60 per cent., respectively, in order to pay such, after all, poor wages of $7 a week to men, $4 a week to women, and $2 a week to children. If we deduct from the value of the production of hosiery in 1880, which was $29,167,227, the amount of wages paid, which was $6,701,475, the balance of production, less wages, would be $22,465,752. Therefore, 30 per cent. is as near as possible the total wages paid on the production. We must certainly assume that Europe pays also wages for the production of hosiery. Suppose we make the extravagant assertion that our wages are double what they are in Europe, which would give a man $3.50, a woman $2, and children $1 a week wages. Of course such wages are ridiculous. But suppose we calculate them as such. Then it follows that the wages for producing $29,167,000 worth of hosiery abroad is only $3,350,000. Therefore, if we tax foreign hosiery 20 per cent. in average instead of 40 and 60 per cent. we would fully protect the home hosiery industry against foreign wages even if the foreign labor only costs half what it costs here. But the most shameful, barefaced outrage in the present duty on hosiery is that up to 1883 the duty on cotton hosiery was 35 per cent. When the Tariff Commission was appointed in 1883, with the avowed intention of reducing the tariff rate 20 per cent., it actually raised the duty on cotton hosiery from 35 to 40 per cent. I suppose the influence of the cotton manufacturers, like the former influence of the slaveholders, was too powerful. Thus does protection imitate slavery, whose twin brother it is. The Southern people of 30 or 40 years ago would neither limit nor reduce slavery. Their motto was "Onward!" carry it to Kansas and the other Territories. The result we see now. The twin brother, protection, has the same motto, "Onward!" always higher duties. Thus they seek to bolster up the rotten system, which is as doomed as slavery was.

JUNE 22, 1887.

LETTER IX.

WHAT IT COSTS TO INDULGE IN THE LUXURY OF COTTON CLOTH.

PROTECTION, that offspring of deception and selfishness, has patented the "lie" that owing to its benign influence manufactured goods are as cheap here as abroad. When confronted with **the fact** that we import $126,000,000 or more of actual manufactured articles ready for use, on which, in 1886, we paid $55,653,000 duty at the rate of 48.9 per cent. ad valorem in average, it crowns the first " lie " with a still bigger one by asserting that this tax is not paid by the American consumers at all. No ! It is the foreign manufacturers who have to pay it. Of course there is a little difficulty in sustaining this falsehood by a simple proof. For instance, England, France, and Germany export ten times more cotton goods of all kinds to such countries as India, China, South America, and other countries, where the duty is only from 4 per cent. to 10 per cent., than they do to the United States. Therefore it would follow that the foreign manufacturer must make two or more prices for his goods for exportation, in order to discriminate or meet the different tariffs.

Thus, if a dozen cotton hose is bought for America the price is $3, but if it is bought for India the price is 35 per cent. more, because the duty in America is 40 per cent. and the duty in India is only 5 per cent. Or, if the same hosiery is bought for home consumption, where there is no duty at all, it should be 40 per cent. dearer than when bought for New York.

How, in this enlightened age, with steam and electricity at our command, with millions of Americans travelling all over the world, such outrageous follies, or say rather palpable falsehoods, can possibly find credence, is the wonder of the age. However, all this corrupt lying and endeavors to rob the people by dire taxation are only so much combustible stored up, which sooner or later will explode as if by spontaneous cumbustion. I will devote this letter to some cotton fabrics so largely used all over the country, and show how outrageously people are taxed.

On page 54 of the official report of imports entered for consumption for 1886 we find the following statistics summarized as to cottons:

	Value of Imports, 1886.	Duty.	Ad valorem per cent.
Cotton cloth, not exceeding 100 threads to the square inch.......	$170,367	$124,304	72.96
Exceeding 100 threads and not exceeding 200 threads............	2,100,735	952,540	45.34
Exceeding 200 threads to the square inch........................	1,459,569	624,951	42.82
Total......................	$3,730,671	$1,701,795	45.62

Now, if there is common-sense still extant in this, the most enlightened country in the world, we ought to reason thus: If, for instance, the same kind of goods is made and sold by our own manufacturers only 10 per cent., or even 5 per cent., cheaper than they cost to import by paying over 45 per cent. duty on them, surely we could not import a single dollar's worth. Hence it follows, inasmuch as we did import $3,730,000, first cost, from abroad, and the people pay more than $5,400,000 for them, that either such goods are not made here at all, or, if made here, that the manufacturer takes the full "pound" of "flesh," that the tariff enhances the foreign manufacture.

Now, if after 26 years of protection this goods cannot be made here, why in the world need there be any duty on it at all, even according to the protection doctrine, inasmuch as the surplus revenue warrants our sparing the duty and lightening the taxes of the people? On the other hand, if this class of goods is largely manufactured in this country, then let us see if we cannot estimate the enormous tax the people pay to Jezebel's favorite god, Baal, or protection (which is all the same).

It seems that the quantity of the above cotton cloth imported, costing, as I stated, $3,730,671 abroad in 1886, was 32,116,890 square yards. Our population in 1886 was at least 60,000,000. In other words, we imported in round numbers something over half a square yard per capita. Now, suppose we say that there were used only three square yards per capita of home-made goods of the same kind, which is a mere flea-bite, or only six times more than was imported. It would naturally follow that a "home tax" exceeding $10,200,000 was paid by the people, besides the $1,701,000 paid into the Treasury. But what is this great luxury on which an average of 45.62 per cent. duty or tax is paid to the Treasury and to home manufacturers? Well, then, the average cost of the 32,116,000 square yards of cotton cloth abroad imported in 1886 was 11⅝ cents a square yard, and the duty on this 11⅝ cents was 5¼ cents.

Now, my friends, the farmers who raise wheat in the West and get about 70 cents a bushel in Chicago for it, or even 75 cents, and have to pay the freight to Chicago, know how hard it is to live at such prices, which probably in some locations does not pay for the raising of it. Anyhow they only get the price prevalent in London less cost for carriage and charges. The planters who raise the very cotton this cloth is made of have to submit to the price paid in Liverpool for the cotton less freight and charges. Is it right, is it honest, that they should be compelled to pay 5¼ cents tax on a square yard of cotton cloth (which, after food, is the most indispensable necessity), that only costs originally 11⅝ cents a square yard? What sophistries, what "lies," can protection possibly bring in palliation of facts officially vouched for and substantiated by the very money paid into the Treasury? But the case is much worse than I stated it. Let the farmers judge for themselves whether a farmer's family, consisting of only, say, seven souls, does not use more than 21 square yards of this cotton cloth during the year. My object is more to point out and demonstrate the wrong and the robbery of protection than to alarm them with the enormity of the hundreds of millions of dollars it costs. Protection, like Saturn, has a keen appetite for devouring its own children. The cotton industry of the United States gives the best proof of it.

Thus we find that in 1860, when there was a low tariff, we exported $11,460,571 worth of cotton fabrics and manufactures, including wearing apparel, while, in 1886, after 35 years of protection and an enormous increase in the production of cotton manufactures, we exported only $13,959,934 of cotton fabrics and manufactures, including wearing apparel, an increase of only $3,000,500. In short, the protected cotton industry despises and snaps its fingers at the foreign export trade. Its mission, like that of Saturn, is to devour its own children at home.

JUNE 30, 1887.

LETTER X.

AN EXAMINATION OF THE TAX ON SPOOL THREAD.

THE tariff is such an immense field, and every article almost that we eat, drink, wear, and use, with but few exceptions, is taxed for some "*other fellow's*" benefit, that really for one who has studied this question during 20 years there is no trouble to find material. In fact, as the French have it, one is perfectly " embarrassed by his riches " to expose the swindle. Let me therefore show now the shameful tax every household pays on such an article as "spool thread." This article, which every woman, and I may say ten-year-old girl, uses in the country, is, according to the definition of Senator Sherman, a great luxury. The worthy Senator stated that our tariff is so harmoniously arranged that we only tax luxuries used by the rich, and that necessities are either free or very lightly taxed. Well then, inasmuch as the tax on spool thread in 1886 was 55.22 per cent. it ought to be considered a luxury. Of course, it is a little awkward for the Ohio statesman, because I believe there is not one sane person in the country who would not at once insist upon spool thread as a necessity and which is universally used by the people. But, then, when a statesman who has served his country for, say, 30 years and has been for many years Chairman of the Senate Finance Committee, where tariffs are made, Secretary of the Treasury, where tariffs are supposed to be the peculiar stock in trade, and applicant these many fruitless years for nominee for the Presidency, even great statesmen get a trifle muddled.

Nevertheless my readers, especially the farmers and their good wives and daughters, will surely consider spool thread a necessity. Now, then, the cost of a dozen spool thread abroad of the best kind, having 200 yards thread on each spool, is about 13d., or, say, almost 27 cents our money. On this amount we exact a duty of 14 cents a dozen. That is, 7 cents a dozen n spool thread that has not more than 100 yards per spool, and 14 cents on all over 100 yards and not over 200 yards per spool. But it must not be supposed that the Treasury gets any considerable revenue from this article of necessity. In fact in 1886 we only imported $78,393 worth of spool thread, and paid a revenue of $43,298 on it, but we also collected $106,508 revenue on the finest kind of yarn, which mostly was used for winding on the spools. Thus the Treasury got altogether about $184,800 revenue from spool thread and cotton yarn going into the production of spool thread. It is difficult to estimate the consumption of spool thread in the United States. But suppose we underestimate it ever so much, and say the per capita use is only three spools, which would be 180,000,000 single spool thread of 200 yards, or 15,000,000 dozen, on which this country pays a tax of 14 cents per dozen, or in the aggregate $2,100,000. Of course this is probably not more than half what is actually used, considering the cloaking, shirts, and all other articles of use that spool thread enters into. But suppose we take this low estimate.

We find then that the division is thus: The Treasury gets a revenue of $184,800, and the people pay a tax of $2,100,000. Of course I will be put down at once by my Scotch friends, the spool-thread manufacturers of this country, as a "Wat Tyler." But let me reassure them. For the present I would certainly not advocate free spool thread. But what I do advocate is a lower duty on this article of necessity. **Surely** a duty of over 55 per cent. on this article is an outrage. I therefore maintain a 30 per cent. duty, or say even 8 cents specific on a dozen spool thread of 200 yards on each spool is quite ample to protect the home industry. My good Scotch friends should remember that we are all God's children. Sixty million people ought to have a voice in this little affair. True, the farmer using, say, only three dozen of spool thread in his household would save at the lower duty but 18 cents a year. Nevertheless, unless we are prepared to entirely hold the poor girl blameless when she pleaded in mitigation that the baby was only a "mite," we must certainly come to the conclusion that an oppressive tax, even if ever so little, is a shame and disgrace, especially if it is taken from the multitude and put into the pockets of perhaps only a dozen rich corporations. Besides the greatest of all objects in view is to break up this infernal system of class taxation, and a tax on spool thread, if it is as high as 55 per cent., is a shame and outrage.

July 20, 1887.

LETTER XI.

THE EFFECT OF THE DUTY ON SILK GOODS.

I SHALL treat now on one of the most important articles of universal use, which the Ohio statesman, Senator Sherman, will, *par excellence*, style a luxury. First of all, let me state that the article I am about to treat in this communication is manufactured silk. And I will prove that this commodity is " not " a luxury.

In 1880, the census year, this country produced $34,519,000 worth of manufactured silk goods. And it is fair to assume that at present the production is at least $40,000,000 worth net. We imported in 1886 silk goods costing abroad $28,055,854, on which a duty was paid into the Treasury amounting to $13,938,096. It therefore follows that the consumption of manufactured silk in this country is as follows:

>   Home-made silk................ $40,000,000
>   Cost of imported silk............   28,055,854
>   Duty paid on importation........   13,938,096
>
>   Total $81,993,950

Surely, on the very face of these figures, it must be admitted that this article is of such universal use that it really has become a necessity. It is perfectly true if the 25,000,000 souls comprising the farming population of this country are to be degraded to the standard of the Russian peasants, then the use of silk goods is a luxury. But to charge an American farmer, whose greatest aim is to see his family decently dressed, of using $10 or even $20 worth of silk in his family, comprising, say, a wife and two daughters, during a year, with being extravagant and indulging in an inordinate luxury, is simply cruel in the extreme, and calls for the proper resentment from a class of citizens who have made and are making this country rich. I admit that a silk dress can become the height of luxury. For instance, if a bloated protectionist's wife or daughter goes to Worth in Paris and orders a silk dress for, say, $500 or even $1000, to be so fashionably made that the party wearing it is exquisitely dressed " only " because she is half undressed, then, of course, silk is a luxury.

But how in the world can 15 yards of black silk, costing in France or Germany say 75 cents, or even $1 a yard, be called a luxury? Considering, too, that the making up of such a dress costs the farmer's wife perhaps $2 or $3 only. Of course the artist at Worth's will despise the making up, especially as the farmer's wife will be fully clad, and not be like the modern fashionable " Eve " in a Parisian paradise or at a levée at St. James's. Well, then, as the wearing and use of silk in the United States is a necessity, what reason is there that a tax of 50 per cent. should be paid on it?

The American farmer sells the surplus of his wheat in Europe; part of it is consumed, say, by the silk-workers abroad. The farmer has to sell his wheat in competition with the wheat-producers of Russia and India. In the latter country the price of labor is about 5 rupees ($2.50) or less a month, and the laborer has to find his own living. Yet the American farmer has to compete with this truly pauper labor of Russia, Turkey, and India, and the worst of it , that the home price of wheat in America is made in Mark Lane, in London. Therefore, selling as our farmer does his product at the lowest price current, why should he be taxed 50 per cent., when in Chicago, Springfield, or anywhere else in the United States he wants to convert a certain quantity of wheat into a certain quantity of silk goods? We can all understand the necessity of such a tax if this country had a heavy interest on the national debt to pay, or had armies in the field—in short, if war taxes were imperative. But when the national trouble and anxiety is how best to reduce the revenue, is not such a tax a national disgrace and a curse upon the people?

Of course the silk manufacturers of this country, who, by the bye, are not very numerous, but immensely rich, will certainly not look upon it in the same light. But this scandal has to end somehow. The raw silk, or the silk manufacturer's raw material, is free. Why should there be a duty of 50 per cent. on manufactured silk? Now, in order (as I have often said in these letters) not to be called a "Watt Tyler," I will simply say I do not advocate free silk goods. But I do advocate a reduction of duty on silk goods, and maintain that 30 per cent. is more than ample not only to protect the home silk manufacturers, but even, if they have the skill and understand their business, to keep foreign importations out of our market, and here I will prove it.

As I have already stated, in 1880, during the census year, which was a year of prosperity and high wages, the American home silk industry produced $34,519,000 worth "net" of silk goods. All the wages paid for this production was $9,146,705. Now, if we deduct the wages from the value of the finished product, we get in round numbers $25,373,000. Thus, then, as the American silk manufacturer gets his raw material free, the same as the European, the only bone of contention is the aristocratic wages of America against the pauper wages of Europe. Well, then, I will be so liberal with my protectionist friends in the silk manufacturing as to astonish them. I will assume that the wages here are double those of France, Germany, and Switzerland. Hence it would follow that the foreign producer would only have to pay $4,573,000 as wages on a similar quantity of goods, and the foreigner's goods would cost $29,946,000, while the American product costs $34,519,000. If we add 30 per cent. duty or protection on $29,946,000, the sum is $8,983,800, and the calculation would stand thus:

> Excess of wages paid in America... $4,573,000
> Protection on $29,946,000 goods... 8,983,800

Or a 30 per cent. duty will, after an allowance of double wages in America, still leave the manufacturers of silk goods about 15 per cent. net profit. But what are the real facts about these aristocratic wages in the silk trade in America? I find that in 1880 all the hands employed were:

Men...................................... 9,375
Women above 16 years old............... 16,396
Children................................. 5,566

Suppose the aristocratic wages of the men, many of whom were no doubt skilled artisans, averaged $9 per week, the wages of the women above 16 years $5 a week, and the wages of the children $1.50 a week, then the sum total would be as follows:

```
9,375 men, on an average, $9 a week....$4,387,500
16,396 women, on an average, $5 a week.  4,262,960
5,566 children at $1.50 a week..........    434,148
                                         ----------
Total..........................          $9,084,608
```

Only about $62,000 less than was actually paid. Now, I leave it to everybody who has to pay 50 per cent. tax on the use of silks whether $5 a week for a grown-up girl or married woman who has to pay for board and lodgings, to find clothes, etc., is aristocratic wages; or whether $9 a week on an average for men, many of whom must be skilled mechanics, is high wages. As for the children in a silk-mill at $1.50 a week wages, the less said the better.

And now I solemnly aver, and will stake my reputation as an economist on the result, that a reduction of duty on silk fabrics from 50 per cent. to 30 per cent. will by no means either flood this market with foreign silk goods, nor will the importation decrease the home production. Thus we find that during the fiscal year of 1883, when the duty on manufactured silks was 60 per cent., our importation amounted to $33,307,112, and the home silk manufacturers imported $14,042,696 worth of raw silk, while in 1886, when the duty had been reduced to 50 per cent. and had been three years in force, the importation of manufactured silk goods was $28,055,854, or $5,250,000 less than in 1883 at 60 per cent., and the importation of raw silk in 1886 was nearly $18,000,000, or $4,000,000 more than in 1882.

Can these facts and deductions be ignored? It is simply a legal robbery that will take a tax of $5 out of the farmer's pocket for the use of $15 worth of silk and put it either into the Treasury, where it forms an embarrassment, or into the pockets of the home monopolist, who morally has no right to it. Here is another chance for the Protective League, whose income is $100,000 a year, and whose mission is to "*lay out*" all those who expose the tariff robbery—to "*lay me out.*" Priests of Baal ! or of high protection, dare you, in the face of the official returns of the census of 1880, the wages of the hands employed in the manufacture of silks which I have given—dare you still uphold this tariff robbery and lay the cause of it to the high and aristocratic wages paid in America ? Why not tell the truth, and say that, if the duty is reduced from 50 to 30 per cent., the few home silk manufacturing corporations will have their annual profits reduced by some $4,000,000 or $5,000,000? All the protective leagues in the world, and all the princely

revenue that they expend or will expend, will not be able to justify the present American tariff. As for the protection literature, leaflets, and all other seductive paraphernalia that the bloated monopoly may use, all I can say is, "the thicker the grass the easier it is mowed."
JULY 28, 1887.

LETTER XII.

FEMALE LABOR ON FARMS AND IN FACTORIES.

I MEAN now to demonstrate to my friends the farmers the undoubted fact that, far from the most protective policy that the world has ever seen during a quarter of a century in this country elevating and bettering the condition of the working classes, it has had the tendency of degrading domestic life, and putting labor and hardships on those that are the least able to bear them. First, I will compare the female labor in factories of this country, in 1860, under 14 years of a revenue tariff, with that in 1880, under 20 years of a protective tariff.

In 1860, after 14 years of a revenue tariff, this country employed in manufactories the following hands, namely:

Males above 15 years old............ 1,040,349
Females above 15 years old.......... 270,897

Now, I call the attention of my readers to

the most significant fact that in the factory labor under a revenue tariff no hands—whether male or female, according to the official statistics—were employed below the age of 15 years. Now let us turn to the year 1880, after 20 years of blessed protection, which, it is claimed, made this nation happy:

> In 1880 there were employed in manufactories, males above 15 years.... 2,025,335
> Females above 15 years............ 531,639
> Children from 10 to 15............. 181,921

In the first place, we find that protection has naturally doubled the hands employed. But it has, unfortunately, nearly doubled the female labor, viz.: from 270,897 in 1860 to 531,639 in 1880. If protection is such a blessing and gives full work and good wages to fathers of families and husbands, why should the female labor double? Besides this, what a sham, swindle, and disgrace is a protective tariff which has enlisted 181,921 children under the age of 15 years to work in factories? Is it not as clear as sunshine that this slaughter of the innocents of 181,000 children in the factories is simply for the purpose of having cheap labor? If these 181,000 children were not allowed to be employed, would not their places have to be taken by persons above the age of 15 years, who naturally would get higher wages? Again, by employing 531,639 women the factories are only employing cheap labor. Of what earthly use is a protection of 80, 90, and even 100 per cent. on woollen goods, or 40, 50, and even 70 per cent. on cotton goods, if we have to employ the same class of labor which, when it is employed in Europe, we sneer down as pauper labor? Has not this protective tariff proved a curse by introducing the employment of children at all? We have it on statistical record that no children below 15 years old were employed in factories before 1861, and anybody who chooses to consult the census returns of 1880 can find that fact in the compendium, volume 2, page 930.

And now as to the employment of females. Let me show the contrast between the farmer's employment of female labor and the employment of female labor by the pampered protective industries.

The farmers in 1880 employed in the United States and Territories

Male laborers	7,075,983
Female labor	594,510

which is a little over 7½ per cent. The manufacturers employed

Males above 15 years old	2,025,335
Females above 15 years old	530,639

which is about 21 per cent., besides the 181,000 children.

But this is not all. Of the agricultural employment of the 594,510 females we find that the 11 cotton-producing States, namely, Alabama, Arkansas, Florida, Georgia, Louisiana, Mississippi, North Carolina, South Carolina,

Tennessee, Texas, and Virginia, employed 537,314 females, which, as every American will understand, is colored labor by females who for the last 250 years have been, as it were, to the manor born, and who, after all, are mostly employed in picking cotton, which compares to the close labor in the walled factories as roast beef compares to oatmeal cakes. Anyhow, we find that the farmers who live in the West and Southwest and produce our breadstuffs, cattle, and dairy products only employed in 1880 57,196 females as laborers on their farms. All honor to the farmer. He does not look for cheap female labor. He does not press children of a tender age into employment. He pays full and manly wages, and treats his white help as his equal. I speak of course of those millions of farmers employed in raising breadstuffs, dairy produce, etc. But they are taxed by those of their fellow-citizens who employ weak women and children of tender age, and who by the grace of a protective tariff make them pay 50 per cent. in average more on nearly all manufactured articles they use on their farms and in their households.

The other day Senator Dawes made a speech at the paper manufacturers' meeting. The worthy Senator is a famous protectionist and took occasion to deplore the inadequacy of protection on worsted goods. Now, it is a fact that in the worsted mills in the United States there were employed in 1880 the following hands:

Males above 15 years.................. 6,435
Females above 15 years................ 9,473
Children less than 15 years........... 2,895

This is an edifying exhibit, is it not? when we find an industry that employs double as many women and children as men. Of course, the reason is simple, cheap labor is sought for and got. Well, then. The Senator, as I said, deplored the inadequacy of the tariff on worsted goods and wants the duty raised, which in other words mean that the people in general, and the farmer in particular, who use most of the worsted goods, shall pay a higher price for it. Now, my worthy friends—I mean you, the tax-ridden farmers—what do you suppose is actually the duty on worsted goods under the present tariff! Let me enlighten you.

In 1886 I find by the Government returns that the duty on worsted goods, either partially of worsted or wholly made of worsted, was 82.18 per cent. and 68.15 per cent. Now, would anybody conversant with these facts believe that a higher duty should actually be demanded by a Senator of the United States? You farmers, who have seen a shrinkage in the price of your wheat within four years from $1.10 in average in Chicago to 68 cents per bushel at present—and it may be to even 65 cents before this year is out—are actually asked to pay more than 82 per cent. and more than 68 per cent. tax respectively on the different kinds of worsted goods that your cold climate in winter makes a necessity. Can assurance, nay, brazen impudence, go further?

When your wheat and corn go down in price, because you have to compete with the truly pauper labor of India, Russia, Turkey, and Egypt, you must grin and bear it. But when it comes for you to buy a necessary woollen garment for the winter, then 82 per cent. tax is not sufficient, and more taxes are demanded. And yet you have it in your own hands to stay this oppression. If you were any way outspoken in your demand that this curse of protective taxation should cease, then would protection, like its original ancestor, Lucifer, be hurled from its present high place to that bottomless pit where it belongs.

AUGUST 4, 1887.

LETTER XIII.

THE TAXES ON COTTON-TIES.

IT is boasted by the protection oligarchy that the Southern people are very fast becoming protectionists. To me it looks like miscegenation to see such a hankering after protection by a people whose very existence depends upon producing 6,000,000 bales of cotton, the price of which is made in Liverpool. Happily this sentiment is only confined to a few frothy advocates in Georgia and Alabama whose economical vision is as blind as was the financial vision of those who cried themselves hoarse for rag money.

It is my purpose to-day to show the planters of Georgia and Alabama how they are oppressed and swindled in paying a tax on cotton-ties. Now, it is an astounding fact that there is not one planter out of ten thousand who does not believe, when he sells a bale of cotton, that he does not get 10 cents a pound paid for the wrapping and steel bands that tie up the bale. Four years ago I had the same controversy with now Senator Chace, of Rhode Island, when happily I was the means of saving the South a tax of 2½ cents a pound on cotton-ties, although the tax is still 35 per cent. ad valorem.

But first of all let me convince the Southern planter that he does not get one single cent paid for the bagging or ties, whether he sells his cotton here or in Liverpool. The fact is perfectly simple. Cotton is sold in the United States by gross weight. That is, if a bale of cotton weighs 450 pounds and the price agreed upon is 10 cents a pound the seller receives $45. In Liverpool, on the other hand, 24 pounds and sometimes 26 pounds tare is deducted; and a bale of cotton weighing 450 pounds only nets, after deducting 24 pounds, 426 pounds, for which the seller is paid. This tare is deducted for the wrapping and the iron or steel ties. Now, then, let us take the price of spot cotton of, say, Sept. 6, both in New York and Liverpool, and we will find the problem solved. The price of spot cotton on the 6th of September in New York was 10 cents per pound, and in Liverpool it was 5 7-16d. per pound.

Proceeds of a bale of cotton weighing 450 pounds in New York, gross, at 10 cents a pound, is $45.

Proceeds of a bale of cotton weighing 450 pounds, gross, in Liverpool, deducting 24 pounds tare, or leaving 426 pounds, at 5 7-16d., is a fraction over £9 13½d., or, exchange at $4.84, is as near as possible $46.71 for the selfsame bale and weight which brings in New York $45, leaving $1.71 per bale for freight and charges.

Thus, if the planter is not purblind, he will see that whether he sells his cotton gross in New York, and is supposed to get paid for the wrapping and ties at the price of cotton, he simply gets the Liverpool price for a bale after the tare of 24 pounds is deducted from it. In other words, he no more gets paid for the wrapping and ties in either country than he gets for the ginning of it. It is entirely a loss to him, and has to be borne by him. This being a mathematical demonstration, the main question is, Why should the planter pay a tax of 35 per cent. on cotton ties when he has to lose the whole cost and value of these ties?

In 1886 the Treasury collected no less than $211,188 duty on cotton-ties, and the account stands thus:

First cost of ties imported in 1886........$603,394
Duty paid on them at 35 per cent......... 211,188

Total lost to the planters.............$814,582

besides the cotton ties bought of the home manufacturer, which were of course enhanced 35 per cent. When the Yankee fisherman needs foreign salt for curing his fish no tax or duty is charged; such is and has been the law for many years. And yet, when the Yankee fisherman sells his dried codfish by weight, he actually does get paid for the salt that the fish contain. But when the planter has to give the cotton-ties to the buyer for nothing he is charged by our swindling tariff 35 per cent. tax. Can outrage or oppression invent a more refined tax cruelty than this? All I wish to make plain to the millions of the Southern planters is that the present tariff is a swindle on their industry; that what they produce they have to sell at the lowest price prevailing in foreign countries, and on what they are obliged to buy for their use they have to pay a tax averaging 44 per cent. That is now the main issue.

SEPTEMBER 10, 1887.

LETTER XIV.

TO MY FRIENDS, THE FARMERS OF THE UNITED STATES: A SUMMING UP.

IN a series of papers I have shown up the hardships that the present villainous tariff imposes on you—a tariff system conceived and enacted during four years of a civil war, and which during 22 years of peace was always altered and amended in the interest of monopoly and restriction. For more than 20 years the great tariff swindle has been like an incubus upon this fair land. To the economist it passes all comprehension how the American farmers, whose industry, sobriety, intelligence, and I may say religious habits, are the pride and mainstay of this great country, now counting more than 60,000,000, could have for so many years acquiesced and borne the hardship of such a villainous, excessive taxation as our present tariff imposes on them.

Well may the economist stand aghast when he considers how anxious the farmer is to get 2 or 3 cents a bushel more for, say, 100 bushels of wheat he has for sale, which at the utmost only amounts to $3 difference; and yet when he has to expend only one-quarter of the sum he receives for 100 bushels of wheat in Iowa or Kansas—say, for instance $18 all told —in winter dresses for his wife and daughters, he actually pays over $8 in taxes on account of the tariff, besides the profit that the several merchants make on the goods. And that there may be no mistake about this statement, let me once more reiterate and prove it by facts and figures. In 1886 we imported 25,200,570 square yards of mixed woollen goods, which cost about $5,377,092.28, or an average of $21\frac{1}{3}$ cents per square yard. On this our tariff exacted a duty of $4,418,888.21, or as nearly as possible 82 18 per cent. That is to say, there was a tax of over 17½ cents on a square yard of woollen dress goods that cost abroad 21⅓ cents. Add to this that the Treasury is actually cursed with a surplus of $100,000,000 annually, and the wonder that such a gigantic tax extortion can exist is beyond all comprehension. Of course this is only a single item in the tax list, as I have already shown more in detail how this tax system presses all the farming population in every article they have to buy and consume, while the surplus agricultural products they raise they have to sell at home at the lowest price prevalent in London and Liverpool. But Congress is about to assemble, and we may fairly expect that the President and the Secretary of the Treasury will call attention to the excessive taxation of the country and the dangerously large surplus accumulating in the Treasury. Both will no doubt strongly recommend a reduction of taxes. But party feelings and the enormous influence of bloated monopolies will strive as much as possible to prevent a reduction of taxes on your necessary clothing, sugar, iron, etc., and offer you free whiskey, free tobacco, and free beer, three essential articles, in the indulgence of which you may forget that enormous taxation which enriches the invested monopolies. Yet you have but to speak, you have but to say in the language of the poet, "A plague on both your parties." Reduce taxes on clothing and necessaries which we must have and consume, and the opposition to the reduction of tariff taxes will melt like snow in an April sunny day. There is an old legend extant—" That the Queen of Sheba was exceedingly handsome, but that she had legs and feet made of potter's clay." Our deceitful monopolies, like the Queen of Sheba, are similarly deformed. And yet they impose their laws, their extortions, with an assurance and tyranny that ignorance and abject fear alone can bring about. Let me expose this virago, with her legs and feet of potter's clay. In 1880 the population of the United States was 50,155,783 souls all told. There were in the same period 17,392,099 wage-earners. That is to say, 32,763,684 depended and lived from the earnings of the 17,-392,099 wage-earners, or, in other words, every wage-earner had on an average to provide a living for himself and two more besides.

The wage-earners in 1880 were divided thus:

Agriculture	7,670,493
Professionals and personal services	4,074,238
Engaged in manufacturing and mining	3,837,112
Engaged in trade and transportation	1,810,256
Total	17,392,099

If we deduct the 3,837,112 wage-earners engaged in manufacturing, who alone maintain that the high tariff tax is necessary for the great welfare of the country, we find that 13,-554,987 wage-earners are very little interested in or benefited by the tariff. On the contrary, they have to work and toil to pay high taxes to the monopolists for the privilege of wearing low-priced clothes, or for the use of iron and steel, or any other manufactured necessaries that they must use. These 13,554,987 wage-earners have to support, including themselves, over 40,000,000 souls, and these 40,000,000 souls are simply the veritable tax serfs to protection. Now, is it even known to one out of a thousand of our people that there were in 1880 237,126 more people employed in professional and personal services than in all our manufacturing and mining industries? Or that there were twice as many wage-earners employed in agriculture as in manufactures? Is it not as plain as daylight that this impudent Queen of Sheba, otherwise monopoly, simply imposes with her brazen pretensions upon 40,000,000 people? Of course we are now 60,000,000 population, and the proportions will only show the worse.

My friends, the farmers, look well at this exposé. Behold how this mighty Queen of Sheba stands on her legs and feet made of potter's clay. And yet the Fiftieth Congress is not asked to abolish all tariff taxes. All that is really now asked is a modification of taxes, which are from 50 to 160 per cent., and cannot be justified in any possible way, except that monopoly must be sustained and made a permanent institution in this free country. This is not a question of party politics. It is simply a question whether after 22 years of peace and when the Treasury is overflowing with a surplus of $100,000,000, the people should pay war taxes for the benefit of monopoly.

DECEMBER 1, 1887.

LETTER XV.

THAT AWFUL SURPLUS.

THERE is no word in the English language which is at this moment more frequently used or quoted than the word *surplus*. Bankers, merchants, brokers, restaurateurs, tailors, and all other bipeds up-town and down-town seem to be troubled about the " surplus in the Treasury." The greatest trouble to all these good people seems to be that the Secretary of the Treasury does not let the *surplus* come out of the Treasury fast enough. Had the Republicans been still in power what a witticism it would have been for them to say that the possession of the Treasury for four weeks only by the Democrats would soon not only dispose of the surplus, but even of the $100,000,000 trust money held for the redemption of the greenbacks. As it is, these awful Democrats, now actually in power, are so careful of the public money that they treat it as a public trust.

Nevertheless, the whole country agrees that the "surplus" in the Treasury is detrimental to business and is likely to lead to great financial and industrial misfortunes. But even the worst enemies to the Democratic Party would not want to see the surplus money once in the Treasury used in a reckless manner, such as loaning it out on wild-cat bonds or stocks. The time for using the surplus by depositing it in some one favorite National Bank has indeed gone by. The Cleveland Administration does not seem to have such an institution hanging about it. And so it happens that the whole financial situation of the country suffers from tight money because the Treasury will not listen to the empirics, by getting rid of some $100,000,000 in a doubtful or unlawful manner. Now, how can intelligent and reasonable people blame the Secretary of the Treasury or the Administration for honestly administering the money in the Treasury ? Is it not a shame and disgrace that such a large surplus should lie in the Treasury ? Can any honest man deny that this vast accumulation of money, which, under present circumstances, must remain locked up, came into the Treasury by dint of excessive taxation? Is it not a national crime to exact war taxes in time of peace ? We imported during the fiscal year 1886-7 five commodities from which we exacted (estimated by the returns of 1885-6) no less than $134,232,000 of hard cash in duties, namely :

Friendly Letters to American Farmers.

	Value of Imports.	Duty Collected.	Per cent. Ad Valorem.
Cotton goods	$29,000,000	$11,658,000	40.20
Manufactured woollen goods	45,000,000	30,262,500	67.25
Manufactures of iron and steel	49,200,000	18,641,880	37.89
Manufactures of silks	31,340,000	15,670,000	50.00
Raw sugar, pounds	2,900,000	58,000,000	*
Revenue collected, estimated		$134,232,380	

* Two cents per pound average.

Now, suppose there had been a reduction of 20 per cent. in average, as was proposed by tariff reformers, and which failed of even being considered in the House by all the Republican members, except three, I believe, and some twenty-odd tariff Democrats, who ought to dwell by rights in the Republican camp. That is to say, after such a reduction

	Per Cent.
Cotton goods would still be taxed	32.16
Woollen goods	53.80
Manufactures of iron and steel	30.31
Silk goods	40.00

and raw sugar would be reduced from 2 cents a pound to 1.60 cents a pound. Surely this does not look either like free trade or, indeed, low duties. Well, if there had been exacted 20 per cent. less than the present existing duty on these five commodities the awful surplus in the Treasury would have been reduced over $26,846,000. Of course, if the sugar duty were reduced 40 per cent. instead of 20, we would still get $11,160,000 less revenue, and the total reduction of the surplus would, on the above five commodities, amount to $38,000,000. And if we further extend the free list and abolish $15,000,000 revenue the tariff reduction would be some $53,000,000, which would make such a hole in the surplus that the abolition of the whole internal tax on tobacco would be problematical.

I have shown from time to time the enormous taxes on the necessaries of life. It must not be supposed that whereas the average duty on woollen goods is only 67.25 per cent., that that is a fair statement. The facts are, the duty on common woollen dress goods costing about 22 cents a square yard in average, of which we imported over $17,000,000 in 1886–7, is over 71 per cent.; on woollen cloths of the cheapest kind, only costing 61½ cents a pound abroad, it is 91 per cent.; on common woollen shawls it is 87 per cent., and so on; while on the high-priced goods used by the wealthy classes the duty is not more than 50 per cent., and even less; hence the average of 67.29 per cent. only. And thus it is with iron and steel goods. Steel rails costing abroad $20 a ton are protected by a duty of $17. In short, the tariff swindle has been so often and so fully exposed by me that I need not go into details here. Well, then, does not this present distress of locking up money by taxing people in the most shameful manner simply rest with Congress? This unnecessary taxation is chiefly and solely for the benefit of a few thousand monopolists and corporations, who not only exact, perhaps a thousand million dollars taxes annually from the people for their sole benefit, but also cause in addition the locking up of money in the Treasury to the detriment of trade and the development of the country which is now known by the awful name of the "surplus" in the Treasury. We have it on record that $100,000 annually is subscribed by 1000 protectionists for the purpose of *laying out* all those who dare to preach the gospel of tariff reform, whether such apostles are in Congress, going to Congress, or even out of Congress. This *laying out* oligarchy persist in calling tariff reform free trade, which reminds one of the silly poet who persisted in calling the Earl of Oxford's swans in his park geese. But they nevertheless remained swans.

The "surplus" in the Treasury reminds me of a standing "legend" so well known to the Moslem population in the Orient, which runs as follows: "Once upon a time a poor but very pious Moslem tailor of Damascus, coming home from the mosque one morning early, found at his door a diminutive, emaciated, entirely nude human being. He took the poor creature into his house, gave him something to eat, and at once set to work to stitch together some worthless rags to clothe the nakedness of the object of his charity. He measured the poor creature's height, tailor fashion, and when at night he had finished his job he gave the hastily improvised garment to his guest. In the morning he called the stranger to put on the garment and say his prayers. To the astonishment of the pious tailor he found that the garment was at least 18 inches too short. In fact, the emaciated, diminutive creature had grown 18 inches overnight. The pious tailor was determined not to send the object of his charity three-fourths naked into the street. So he measured him again, making due allowance, and added to the garment the wanting cloth. When next morning he bade his guest put on the altered garment the tailor was awestruck to find the dress again too short, and the diminutive creature he took into his house had grown in two days to an inordinate height. Divining at once that his guest was superhuman, he asked him, naturally, who and what he was. 'Alas!' said he, 'stranger, I am the "Genius of Poverty." When once admitted to human habitation I grow overnight. Now, for your kindness to me let me give you wholesome advice. First, don't try to clothe me, as you will find I shall always outgrow your measure. Secondly, not only get rid of me at once, *but never take me into your house again if you wish to avoid trouble.*'"

Now, this Moslem legend comes in pat with the "awful surplus." Suppose the Treasury gets rid of $30,000,000 of surplus revenue, what of it? As long as we are under the present outrageous, shameful taxation the "surplus" will grow quicker than the Treasury can get rid of it. Suppose the act of March 3, 1881, is literally carried out, it will require the necessary Government bonds to procure the money now locked up. Does it not seem rather strange that with all the outcry of tight money, when $14,000,000 cash has been ready for more than ten days in the Treasury to be exchanged for 4½ and 4 per cent. bonds, yet not much more than half of the money has been absorbed? Therefore, if money is really scarce, Government bonds seem still scarcer. In the meantime the surplus, like the "Genius of Poverty" in the Moslem legend, keeps growing apace, and will grow as long as the people are thus outrageously taxed. Does it really take a *surplus* of brains as well as a surplus of revenue to understand that if the present tax is kept on the surplus will be $200,000,000 in a year or two? Here is one example: In 1884, only three years ago, we consumed 2,437,000,000 pounds of raw sugar and collected a revenue of $47,500,000. During 1886-7 we consumed *over* 2,900,000,000 pounds of foreign sugar and collected $58,000,000 revenue, or, say, $10,000,000 more than three years ago. Does it really require a *surplus* of understanding not to see that you must get from sixty millions of people, if taxed the same on sugar or anything else, more revenue than you can get from fifty-eight millions, and that next year, when there is a million or two perhaps more population, that the revenue must increase with the increase of population? Of course, there is an easy remedy, after which all protectionists, and even financial magnates, who are perhaps interested in home monopolies, hanker. And that is to abolish the internal taxes in toto. Which means—but I'll give you my meaning in a table :

		Per Cent.
Free whiskey.	Tax on sugar	80
Free tobacco.	Tax on rice	112
Free beer.	Tax on salt	83
	Tax on corn starch	93
	Tax on potatoes	45
	Tax on woollen dress goods costing 22 cents a yard	71
	Tax on common cloth	91
	Tax on woollen hosiery	70
	Tax on flannels	72
	Tax on common woollen shawls	87
	Tax on cotton hosiery	45
	Tax on cotton bagging	54
	Tax on plain earthenware	55
	Tax on window-glass	86
	Tax on plate-glass	147
	Tax on steel rails	80

In fact, I can go on with a similar list of necessaries and fill pages. But this will suffice as a specimen. I don't think that outside of Pennsylvania and the few hundred millionaire monopolists the people of this tax-ridden country are inclined to encourage a saturnalia of free intoxicating whiskey and keep up such taxation as I give above.

SEPTEMBER 28, 1887.

LETTER XVI.

OUR VILLAINOUS TARIFF.

MALCOLM—*If such a one be fit to govern, speak.
I am as I have spoken.*
MACDUFF— *Fit to govern!
No, not to live. A nation miserable
With any untitled tyrant bloody-sceptred,
When shalt thou see thy wholesome days again?*

THOSE of you who for more than a score of years have been accustomed to read my letters on tariff reform will do well to read and study the tariff table I give below, compiled from official returns of 1886. This table is indeed a pyramid. My object is to show the enormous high duties exacted by the American tariff on articles of necessity, and then you may judge whether Macduff's answer to Malcolm does not exactly fit our " untitled tyrant bloody-sceptred " tariff system.

Articles on which a Duty of 100 *Per Cent. and Over was Exacted in* 1886.

	Per Cent.
Castor oil	189.28
On tannic and tannin	163.75
Acetate of lead	133.07
Santonine	166.15
Common window-glass over 24 by 30 inches	100.83
Plate-glass over 24 by 60 inches	147.43
Iron beams, girders, and joists	113.91
Ingots, cogged blooms, or blanks	121.89
Galvanized wire smaller than No. 10 and not smaller than No. 16	100.00
Wire cloth smaller than No. 16 and not smaller than No. 26.	103.34
Wire cloth smaller than No. 26	100.13
Horseshoe nails	103.85
Varnish of spirits	106.23
Scoured clothing wool	119.43
Cleaned rice	112.46

Articles that Paid a Duty of 90 Per Cent. and Over and not 100 Per Cent. in 1886.

	Per Cent.
Copperas	94.27
Common window-glass, 16 by 24 inches	92.89
Hoop iron thinner than No. 20	98.97
Corn or potato starch	93.56
Sugar above No. 13 and not above No. 16	91.89
Common woollen cloth costing 61 cents per pound	91.95
Woollen manufactures not costing over 80 cents per pound abroad	91.47

Articles that Paid a Duty of 80 Per Cent. and Over and not 90 Per Cent.

Bicarbonate of soda	88.63
Common cylinder window-glass, 10 by 16 inches, used in the cheapest houses	80.70
Hoop iron 8 inches or less in width	85.81
Sheet iron No. 20, wire gauge	81.30
Litharge (a lead paint)	89.81
Red lead paint	81.24
Whiting and Paris white	89.38
Woollen dress goods costing 21⅓ cents square yard abroad	82.18
Woollen shawls costing 67½ cents a pound abroad	87.00
Steel rails at the average cost of 1886-7	80.00

Articles that Paid a Duty of 70 Per Cent. and Over and not 80 Per Cent.

Boracic acid in crude state	70.13
Bleached cotton cloth costing 5 cents square yard	70.40
Colored cotton cloth costing 6 cents square yard	76.88
Iron less than 1 inch wide	70.30
Sheet iron thinner than No. 25 and not No. 29	76.50
Sheet iron thinner than No. 20 and not 25	74.55
Sheet iron, Anaker class sheet iron	77.81
Iron or steel railway wheels	72.84
Pig lead	74.05
Lead pipes, sheets, and shot	70.60
Orange mineral lead (paint)	71.03
Uncleaned rice	71.72
Raw sugar up to No. 13	70.00
Washed clothing wool	74.97
Scoured combing wool	73.58
Woollen blankets costing 26 cents per pound	73.39
Woollen blankets costing 65 cents per pound	71.64
Common druggets	71.40
Woollen cloaks and dolmans	71.84
Flannels costing not over 30 cents per pound	70.62
Flannels not costing over 40 cents per pound	71.12

	Per Cent.
Flannels costing over 80 cents per pound	72.66
Woollen hosiery not costing over 30 cents a pound	70.60
Woollen yarns valued above 60 cents and not over 80 cents per pound	70.04
Manufactures of wool or worsted valued not over 30 cents per pound	73.82

Articles that Paid Duty of 60 Per Cent. and Over and not 70 Per Cent.

Blue vitriol (sulphate of copper)	65.29
Glycerine refined	66.40
China porcelain, decorated	60.00
Peanuts not shelled	63.90
Rolled or hammered iron 1 by ⅜ inch	63.04
Sheet iron thinner than No. 20 and not No. 25	69.38
Galvanized wire smaller than No. 5 and not No. 10	66.00
Wire rope, No. 10 and not No. 16	61.04
Wire rope, No. 16 and not No. 26	63.38
Cast-iron pipe of every description	66.60
Tiles over 14 inches long	60.68
Umber and umber earth, dry	63.23
Washed raw wool	65.92
Wool blankets valued above 30 cents and not over 40 cents per pound	67.96
Wool blankets valued above 40 cents and not over 60 cents per pound	68.46
Wool blankets valued above 80 cents per pound	65.38
Woollen cloth valued over 80 cents a pound	68.57
Mixed woollen dress goods costing 15 cents square yard	67.85
Mixed woollen dress goods costing 34 cents square yard	60.60
Flannels costing 40 cents a pound	65.00
Flannels costing 69 cents a pound	69.69
Wool hats costing less than 60 cents a pound	65.24
Wool hats costing 60 cents and not over 80 cents a pound	69.39
Wool hats costing over 80 cents a pound	60.79
Woollen hosiery valued above 30 cents and not over 40 cents a pound	68.80
Woollen hosiery over 40 cents and not over 60 cents a pound	69.26
Woollen hosiery over 60 cents and not over 80 cents a pound	68.86
Woollen hosiery valued over 80 cents a pound	60.37
Woollen hosiery valued at 30 cents and not over 40 cents per pound	68.80
Woollen hosiery valued over 40 cents and not over 60 cents per pound	69.26
Woollen hosiery valued above 60 cents and not over 80 cents per pound	68.86
Woollen hosiery valued over 80 cents per pound	60.37
Woollen shawls valued over 80 cents per pound	63.17

	Per Cent.
Woollen shawls wholly or partly of wool	60.37
Woollen yarns costing 30 cents and not over 40 cents per pound	67.00
Woollen yarns valued over 40 cents and not over 60 cents per pound	68.22
Woollen yarns valued over 80 cents per pound	67.57
Manufactures of wool exceeding 80 cents per pound	60.14
Worsted goods valued above 30 cents and not above 40 cents per pound	68.83
Worsted goods valued above 40 cents and not above 60 cents per pound	67.91
Worsted goods valued above 80 cents per pound	61.75
Zinc, in sheets	67.65
Zinc old metal fit only for smelting	69.00

Articles that Paid a Duty of 50 Per Cent. and Over and not 60 Per Cent.

Licorice paste used in manufacturing tobacco	57.49
Cotton yarn valued over 60 cents and not over 70 cents per pound	51.69
Cotton yarn valued over 80 cents and not over $1 per pound.	54.02
Cotton yarn valued above $1 a pound	50.00
Spool thread	55.23
Common cotton cloth costing 8 cents or less a square yard.	56.90
Common cotton cloth exceeding 100 threads and not costing over 8 cents a square yard	50.28
Common cotton cloth exceeding 100 threads costing over 8 cents and not over 10 cents a square yard	54.38
Common cotton cloth exceeding 200 threads valued at 10 cents or less a square yard	51.15
Common cotton cloth, bleached, valued at 12 cents or less a square yard	50.71
Plain white crockery, not painted or ornamented	55.00
All other china or earthenware	55.00
Jute bagging, used for cotton bags	54.06
Honey	55.55
Pig iron	57.72
Scrap iron	55.86
Scrap steel	51.65
Bar iron, rolled, less than $\frac{7}{8}$ inch in diameter	51.65
Bar iron valued 4 cents or less a pound	51.77
Bar of steel costing less than 4 cents a pound	52.27
Bar of steel costing over 4 cents and not over 7 cents a pound.	43.36
Sheet steel valued not over 4 cents per pound	52.29
Sheet steel valued over 4 cents and not over 7 cents per pound.	50.75
Steel wire smaller than No. 10 and not No. 16	50.13
Penknives, pocket-knives, and razors	50.10
Files and rasps 4 inches in length and under	52.61

	Per Cent.
Files and rasps over 4 inches and not over 9 inches	58.66
Files and rasps over 9 inches and not over 14 inches	53.16
Nuts and washers made of steel or iron	57.14
Spikes of wrought iron	51.14
Railway fish plates	56.41
Rivets and bolts	50.32
Old lead fit for melting	53.88
Rough marble	55.90
Marble, veined and dressed	56.66
Croton oil	52.25
Sulphate of barytas	50.90
Ultramarine	53.77
Wood pencils	56.77
Paddy or uncleaned rice	51.02
Castor beans	50.54
Manufactures of silks	50.00
Raw wool, class 1, clothing wool	55.50
Balmoral valued above 80 cents per yard	58.09
Brussels carpets	59.05
Patent velvet carpets	55.53
Saxony and Wilton	55.00
Tapestry	59.36
Ready-made clothing	53.91

I purposely stop this pyramidal tariff swindle at a duty of not less than 50 per cent. It will the better show the tax-ridden people the oppression of the swindling system. I have of course omitted in this table to mention the duties on luxuries, such as wines, spirits, tobacco, cigars, perfumery, etc. I have omitted even kid gloves. I included silk, because the use of it is now so universal in every household in this country that unless the tariff system makes a nation of paupers of this happy land, silks are no more of a luxury than any other moderate-priced article of clothing. This is well understood in every household. Now! my fellow-citizens, the issue is this: You must either make up your minds to sweep away the internal revenue tax and give the people free whiskey, free beer, and free tobacco, and keep the tariff as it is intact, or, you can reform the above robbery by cutting down the tax on clothing and necessaries and tax the drunkards on their whiskey and even beer, although you may remove the tobacco tax. And now, in conclusion, my fellow-citizens, I wish once more to call your attention to the most vital fact, namely, when you are told that this high duty, all the way from 50 per cent. to over 150 per cent., as contained in the above, is necessary on account of the higher wages paid here, such assertions are the most misleading and false. And here let me prove it from the census returns of 1880, a year of high-priced wages:

"*In 1880 the total production of manufactured goods in the United States was, in value, $5,369,579,191. Wages paid to produce the above were $947,953,795, which is less than 18 per cent. of the production.*"

Now, it is plain if our manufactures are protected 18 per cent., and the foreign pauper labor would be entirely gratis, that we would then be even as far as wages go. But, as foreign labor costs something, any protection over, say, 20 per cent. is simply for the enrichment of monopoly. And when such a protection is carried higher even than 50 per cent., then it becomes simply an oppressive tax robbery, and the workingman is made the excuse of the impudent lie that such taxes are necessary for his protection.

OCTOBER 11, 1887.

LETTER XVII.

THE PINNACLE OF THE TARIFF SWINDLE.

"PECCAVI," "peccavi." Who could have supposed that in compiling a list of duties paid in 1886 that the highest duty paid on an article of necessity should have escaped me? How true is the wise proverb which says, "Do not rely on thy knowledge." In first printing this letter, I omitted the tax or duty on castor-oil. But this happily caused me to give my tariff friends a special dose of castor-oil. Here goes! In 1886 we imported 13,644 gallons of castor-oil, costing abroad $5576.61. On this oil the Treasury collected a revenue of $10,915.17, or 189.28 per cent. This high tax was necessary for two reasons. In the first place, it was necessary to protect the "infant" castor-bean growers at the rate of 50.54 per cent. against the pauper castor-beans of India, and inasmuch as the raw material was protected 50 per cent., the "infant" castor-oil crushers took simply a protection of 189 per cent. as a compensation. We all know what castor-oil is used for, although for aught I know it may be used otherwise than medicinally. But no one could possibly maintain that castor-oil is a luxury. Our tariff system is so thoroughly corrupt that there are degrees in this villainous system. For instance, raw wool is the foundation, and raw material of all woollen manufactures. Raw wool was protected, or foreign wool was taxed, in 1886 in average just 56.10 per cent., and manufactured woollen goods were taxed during the same year in average 67.29 per cent. Thus it will be seen that the difference of the tax in the manufactured goods and in the raw material was 11.19 per cent. That is one degree of tariff taxation.

But when we turn to castor-oil, we find quite another story. The castor-beans are taxed 50.54 per cent., and the castor-oil is taxed 189.28 per cent., a difference of 138.74 per cent. And yet even at this outrageous tax the home castor-oil crushers could not prevent the importation of 3,644 gallons of foreign oil, which only proves that home-made castor-oil takes either the full pound of flesh of the tax, or that the foreign oil is so much purer and must be had at any price. It is now in order to show the extent of this mighty home industry known as castor-oil crushing. In 1880 there were just eight establishments engaged in this business. The capital invested was $474,000. The total hands employed were 107 men and 1 boy. The total amount of wages paid was $44,714. The cost of material was $384,890, and the finished product realized or was valued at $653,900.

Now, if we deduct the wages and cost of materials, which together amounted to $429,604, from $653,900, there remains a clear profit of $224,296 on a capital of $474,000. Of course, far be it from me to call in question the correctness of either the capital invested or the value of the finished product. All I want my fellow-citizens to remember is that this statement is made by the castor-oil crushers themselves. Nor would I for the world insinuate that the capital is " watered," or the value of the product " oiled." I only give plain official facts. But by their own showing it would take less then two years and two months to pay for the whole capital invested. But, after all, what does it matter? My esteemed friend, Senator Evarts, would at once show that to pay eight castor oil crushing establishments $224,000 annually is only about three-eighths of a cent tax per capita on 60,000,000 people per annum, and it would be a pity to deprive them of this little " backsheesh."

OCTOBER 25, 1887.

LETTER XVIII.

AS TO LUXURIES AND NECESSITIES.

WHEN a public man, or rather a statesman, who for more than a quarter of a century has filled the places of Congressman, Senator, Chairman of the Senate Finance Committee, and Secretary of the Treasury, speaks on the most important economic question of the day, namely, the tariff, the least that the public has a right to expect is that his statements should be correct, however erroneous his deductions may be. Senator Sherman is reported to have made the following statement in his speech in Springfield, Ill. After referring to the free list, which amounts to one-third of the importation, he said:

"We levied a duty on the remaining two-thirds sufficient to raise all the revenue needed, almost exclusively on articles that competed with home products. In this way we so protected our industries that nearly every article of common use on the farm, in the workshop, or the household is made in this country. Nearly all the articles, except sugar, from which this large revenue is derived, are articles of luxury mainly consumed by the rich."

Now what are the official facts? The ex-Secretary of the Treasury here distinctly states that with the exception of sugar, which he considers happily not a luxury, nearly all other articles from which the customs revenue is derived are articles of luxury, "*mainly consumed by the rich.*"

Let me show how utterly at variance with actual facts his statement is.

Our customs revenue in 1886 was $188,379,-397. If we take from this the revenue collected on sugar and molasses, which amounted to $51,-778,948, the balance of revenue collected from all other products imported would be $136,600,-449.

My object is to show how much of this revenue was derived from luxuries. The duties collected in 1886 from articles which might in a sense be considered luxuries were as follows :

On works of art.....	$629,191
On carriages and parts thereof........	89,728
On clocks and watches..............	356,504
On all fancy articles................	2,456,398
On gold and silver manufactures......	167,575
On jewelry and precious stones........	900,474
On liquors, spirits, and wines..........	7,194,147
On musical instruments..............	358,093
On manufactured silks of all kinds.....	13,938,096
On tobacco and cigars...............	8,311,114
Total........................	$34,401,320

The revenue from customs in 1886 would, therefore, be divided thus :

On articles of necessity..............	$102,199,129
On sugar...........................	51,778,948
On luxuries.......................	34,401,320
Total revenue from customs.....	$188,379,397

With such statistical facts before us, how can Senator Sherman, the most important member of the Senate Finance Committee and ex-Secretary of the Treasury, try to impose on the country a statement that, with the exception of the duty on sugar, the revenue is nearly all derived from articles of luxury mainly consumed by the rich ?

Surely Senator Sherman must know that we collected the following revenue in 1886:

On wool and woollens................	$27,278,527
On cotton manufactures..............	11,752,206
On flax, hemp, and manufactures......	9,247,816
On iron, steel, and manufactures......	14,631,875
On chemicals, drugs, and dyes.........	4,347,626
On fruits...........................	3,498,569
On leather and manufactures.........	3,262,232
On earthenware.....................	2,829,539
On glass and glassware..............	3,694,923
On rice............................	1,184,138
On wood and lumber................	1,423,301
On breadstuff......................	1,042,404
Total revenue on 12 commodities..	$84,193,156

It is no doubt easy enough in a crowded and friendly assembly to make glittering assertions, but it is rather awkward when they can be knocked over like a card-house by mere force of actuals facts.

However, I have no objection to Senator Sherman's flighty statements about the tariff. The thicker the paint is laid on the hideous tariff corpse, the easier it can be exposed.

JUNE 2, 1887.

LETTER XIX.

A NATION MADE HAPPY AND RICH BY HIGH TAXATION.

DR. SANGRADO maintained that the most infallible remedy for all diseases mankind is heir to is simply "bleeding" and lukewarm water.

Strange to say, the patients, notwithstanding this simple and powerful remedy, invariably died. History repeats itself. Senator Sangrado Sherman in his powerful speech in the Senate has laid down as a demonstrated rule, to make a nation happy and rich is to tax all articles of necessity to that high degree which reasonable people would think a calamity. I herewith give an extract of duties exacted on the strict necessaries of life during the year 1886–7, dividing it into two classes—first, taxation of 100 per cent. and over ; second, taxation of not less than 60 per cent. and not over 100 per cent. The result is as follows :

AMOUNT OF DUTIES COLLECTED DURING THE FISCAL YEAR OF 1886–7 ON ARTICLES OF NECESSITY AT 100 PER CENT. AND OVER.

Articles.	Duties Collected 1886–7.	Percentage Ad Valorem, 1886–7
Common window-glass above 16 by 24 and not exceeding 30 inches	$389,974	106.21
All above 24 by 30	506,242	108.50
Plate-glass above 24 by 60	853,367	152.94
Iron or steel beams, girders, joists, etc.	168,920	102.75
Galvanized wire smaller than No. 10 and not smaller than No. 16	1,378	111.18
Wire cloth, No. 16 to 26	272	100.75
Galvanized wire cloth, No. 26	1,032	114.21
Castor oil	1,205	194.77
Whiting and Paris white, dry	6,240	134.01
Rice, cleaned	758,957	113.03
Total at 100 per cent. and over duties collected	$2,687,587	

AMOUNT OF DUTIES COLLECTED DURING THE FISCAL YEAR OF 1886–7 ON ARTICLES OF NECESSITY, NOT LESS THAN 60 PER CENT. AND NOT OVER 100 PER CENT.

Articles.	Duties Collected.	Percentage Ad Valorem.
Bicarbonate of soda	$37,180	81.18
Regulus of copper	1,018	70.57

Articles.	Duties Collected.	Percentage Ad Valorem.
Common cotton cloth costing 4⅝c. a square yard abroad	46,387	75.25
Common cotton cloth costing 6c. a square yard abroad	67,191	73.31
Common window-glass 16 by 24	252,781	93.11
Common window-glass 10 by 15	194,120	60.71
Plate-glass 24 by 60	324,074	78.40
Steel rails	841,667	84.33
Iron wire smaller than No. 26	218	89.94
Cut tacks	3	80.21
Anchors and parts thereof	2,316	68.26
Files over 4 inches and not over 14 inches	18,476	64.97
Files over 14 inches	3,789	63.29
Lead in pigs	222,964	68.97
Horseshoe nails	2,520	76.26
Railway fish plates	254	92.75
Boiler tubes and flues	49,712	70.97
Railway wheels	214,525	78.26
Litharge (lead paint)	1,433	83.54
Orange mineral (lead paint)	48,654	70.00
Red mineral	13,060	76.96
Uncleaned rice	60,009	71.52
Salt in bulk	284,010	79.68
Starch, corn and potato	6,237	94.54
Starch from rice	7,515	97.90
Brown sugar up to No. 13	56,472,072	82.00
Varnish	5,905	95.30
Wool blankets costing 22 cents per pound	661	79.66
Bunting	42	80.75
Druggets	1,000	73.92
Flannels of all kinds	129,674	70.02
Woollen knit goods	1,243,689	62.80
Woollen shawls	654,008	63.50
Woollen yarns	1,207,734	69.11
Woollen cloths	7,055,824	70.40
Woollen dress goods	12,398,974	72.09
Woollen clothing	896,471	61.35
Worsted goods	1,058,004	71.99
All other manufactures of wool	4,560,904	68.52
Chicory root	106,671	65.17
Earthenware	2,165,078	60.00
Axles	19,730	62.29
Total	$90,676,554	

RECAPITULATION.

Duties at 100 per cent. and over.............	$2,687,587
Duties over 60 per cent. and not over 100 per cent....	90,676,554
Total...	$93,364,141

Now, be it remembered by my readers and fellow-citizens that in the above $93,364,141 taxes exacted, first of all they are all commodities used and consumed by the hard-working farmers and wage-earners ; *not one can be styled a luxury.*

And second, none of these articles are taxed less than 60 per cent. Of course, there are plenty of necessities that are taxed 50 per cent. and over. For instance:

	Duty Collected.	Duty Per Cent.
Bar iron...........................	$677,789	50.79
Common earthenware....	1,032,038	55.00
Pig iron...........................	1,801,646	56.60
Cutlery............................	709,930	50.00
Raw clothing wool..................	2,395,536	55.20

And, indeed, many million dollars at the rate of 50 per cent. and over that are too numerous to mention. I did not so far allude to silk fabrics, which are taxed 50 per cent. and yielded a revenue of $15,540,000. Of course I took no notice of wines, liquors, tobacco, and cigars, or any other luxury. But I wish simply to call attention to this legal, shameful robbery, squeezing $93,364,000 taxes out of the people on articles of first necessity, the duty on which at lowest is not less than 60 per cent. and at highest 194 per cent.

Now, who is the people's friend ? Is it the

Executive in the White House, who advises and urges a reduction of these shameful taxes, or the man who resists such reductions and tries to persuade a tax-ridden people to go on paying them, not for the benefit of the Treasury and Nation, but for the sole benefit of bloated home monopolies? Again be it known, understood, and proclaimed, that, far from desiring to put any of the goods named in the list now paying 60 per cent. and over on the free list, all that tariff reform asks is simply a reduction of these enormous taxes, that are oppressive and unjust. For my part I would feel perfectly satisfied to see these articles reduced in duty *not to less than 40 per cent.*

Well may the President leave this issue to the people. Well may tariff reformers laugh at the shrieks of tariff monopoly advocates, that 40 per cent. duty means, and to all intents and purposes is, free trade. The people of this country are all at once wide-awake to the fact that you cannot make a nation "*rich*" and "*happy*" by inordinate taxation; and as Dr. Sangrado died from using his own remedy by being continually bled and by drinking lukewarm water, so will Senator Sangrado Sherman find his political extinction in using his outrageous high tax remedy as a means of obtaining the prize of his highest ambition.

JANUARY 8, 1888.

LETTER XX.

WAR TAXES IN TIME OF PEACE.

It may perhaps be of some use if I select only a few articles in our legal piratical tariff system to show how more than war taxes are exacted in time of peace. On the 3d of March, 1863, which was about as dark a period in the history of this country as can well be imagined—when a million of men were in the field and United States bonds were selling at about 50 cents gold on the dollar—well, on that day a tariff act was passed to lay upon a whole people war taxes which it was fondly hoped were only to be temporary. I give here the war duty of 1863 on only 16 articles (out of some thousands) and put them in the deadly parallel line with the peace duties of 22 years later. Let the reader judge whether our tariff needs revision or not.

War duties passed March 3, 1863, when a million soldiers were in the field on both sides, and when American 6 per cent. gold bonds sold at 50 cents gold on the dollar.	War duties in 1886, after 21 years of peace, when the surplus revenue is from $50,000,000 to $100,000,000, and our 4 per cent. bonds sell at 124.
Cotton, unbleached, less than 100 threads to the square inch, 1¼ cents square yard..................	2½ cents square yard.
Cotton, bleached, less than 100 threads to the square inch, 1¾ cents square yard......................	3½ cents square yard.
Colored and printed, 2½ cents square yard................................	4½ cents square yard.
Over 100 threads, unbleached, 2½ cents square yard..................	3 cents square yard.
Over 100 threads, bleached, 3 cents square yard......................	4 cents square yard.

War duties passed March 3, 1863, when a million soldiers were in the field on both sides, and when American 6 per cent. gold bonds sold at 50 cents gold on the dollar.	War duties in 1886, after 21 years of peace, when the surplus revenue is from $50,000,000 to $100,000,000, and our 4 per cent. bonds sell at 124.
Cotton yarn, 35 per cent............	47 per cent. average.
Earthenware, common, 20 per cent..	25 per cent.
Earthenware, printed, painted, and decorated, 35 per cent............	55 per cent.
Porcelain, ornamented, 40 per cent..	60 per cent.
Woollen hosiery, 35 per cent........	from 58 per cent., lowest, to 69 per cent.
Woollen cloaking, 18 cents per pound and 30 per cent...................	40 cents per pound and 35 per cent.
Woollen cloak and cassimere, 18 cents per pound and 30 per cent........	35 cents per pound and 35 per cent.
Raw wool, combing, and cloaking, 9 cents per pound...................	10 cents and 12 cents per pound.
Pig iron, $6 per ton................	$6.75.
Bar iron, rolled and hammered, $17.	$17.92 per ton.
Iron ore, 10 per cent...............	24 per cent. in average.

Of course, I could carry this list up in the same degree to some hundreds or even thousands. But the above example will suffice.

Slavery and serfdom have existed in this world for thousands of years, and they have only one characteristic, and that is that either the strong tyrants or the still more dangerous cunning tyrants (who are comparatively only very few) shall tax the multitude, be it either in labor or taxes, for their benefit. Slavery is now and forever impossible in this free country. But the cunning tyrants who oppress the multitude by dint of false assertions and by artfully devised hidden laws are still rampant and in full force. Let my above table demonstrate this truth.

OCTOBER 11, 1887.

LETTER XXI.

THE CHAMPION TARIFF SWINDLE OF THE WORLD.

THERE are many Christmas books, pamphlets, and leaflets published that in general are more amusing than useful. Allow me, my fellow-citizens, to present you with a brief collection of statistics that will, I am sorry to say, be more useful than amusing. I herewith give an extract of only a small number of articles that may be called luxuries and others that certainly are necessaries of life which I place in parallel columns to show how they are respectively taxed by the present tariff, and without further preface, here they are:

Duty on Articles of Luxury.	*Duty on Articles of Necessity.*
Ottar of roses, free.	Castor oil, 180 per cent.
Neroli or orange flower oil, free.	Linseed oil 62 per cent.
Diamonds, 10 per cent.	Common window-glass, 87 per ct.
Raw silk, free.	Raw wool, 45 per cent.
Jewelry, 25 per cent.	Steel rails, 85 per cent.
Gold studs, 25 per cent.	Horseshoe nails, 116 per cent.
Finest still wines, in bottles, 29 per cent.	Cheapest mixed woollen goods, costing abroad 24 cents per yard, 77 per cent.
Finest thread lace, 30 per cent.	Spool thread, 51 per cent.
Fine Aubusson and Axminster carpets, costing abroad $2.77 a yard, 46 per cent.	Common druggets, costing abroad 26 cents a yard, 86 per cent.
Finest India shawls, costing abroad, say $20 a pound weight, 35 cents a pound and 40 per cent. ad valorem, or say 40½ per cent.	Common woollen shawls, costing abroad 68 cents a pound, 86 per cent.

Duty on Articles of Luxury.	*Duty on Articles of Necessity.*
Silk stockings, 50 per cent.	Common worsted stockings, costing 26 cents a pound abroad, 73 per cent.
Finest broadcloth, costing $5 a pound abroad, 35 cents a pound and 40 per cent., equal to about 41 per cent.	Common cloth, costing 65 cents a pound abroad, duty 35 cents a pound and 35 per cent. ad valorem, equal to 89 per cent.
Pâté de foie gras, 25 per cent.	Rice, 106 per cent.
Musical instruments of all kinds 25 per cent.	Galvanized wire smaller than No. 16 and not smaller than No. 26 wire gauge, 132 per cent.; smaller than No. 26, 155 per cent.
Duty on a quart bottle of champagne, costing abroad $1 a bottle, 58 cents.	Duty on a dollar's worth of bleached cotton fabric, costing abroad 5¼ cents a square yard, 66¼ cents.
Curry and curry powder, free.	Potatoes, 15 cents duty per bushel.
Olives, green or prepared, free.	Corn starch, 85¼ per cent. duty.
Spices of all kinds, free.	Salt, 85 per cent. duty.

Of course this is only a drop in the bucket of thousands of other items that might be treated in a similar manner. And now I challenge the journals who uphold our tariff system,

First—To print the above list, which represents the greatest legal swindle of the age. And.

Second—To explain and vindicate the justice of retaining these enormous taxations. I wish further to remind you, my fellow-citizens, that when the question came up in the House to consider, remember, I say, "*consider*," the advisability of reducing these taxes, 154 members of Congress (composed of 131 Republicans and 23 Democrats) maintained by their vote that the question should not even be considered. Remember, further, that for the $200,000,000 customs revenue that goes into the Treasury you, my fellow-citizens, pay at least $1,000,000,000 into the pockets of monopolists every year. I regret that I shall spoil your Christmas cheer. But if reason, common-sense, fair play, and independence, which ought to be the distinguishing marks of the American citizen are not entirely subdued, this very little Christmas present may prove more useful to the future welfare of this free land than anything that you could possibly have received during the year. There was a time in this country when such uncontradicted wrong and legal robbery was properly and lawfully resented. How much of this spirit of freedom and independence is left in the present generation to lift up not their hands, but their voices, in defence of their rights, it is for you to decide.

DECEMBER 22, 1886.

www.ingramcontent.com/pod-product-compliance
Lightning Source LLC
Chambersburg PA
CBHW020152170426
43199CB00010B/1002